Local Distinctiveness

Place, Particularity and Identity

Local Distinctiveness

Place, Particularity and Identity

Essays for a conference
September 28, 1993

Edited by
Sue Clifford and Angela King

Common Ground

Published by Common Ground 1993
41 Shelton Street, Covent Garden, London WC2H 9HJ

The collection © Common Ground, 1993

The Essays © the Contributors 1993

ISBN: 1-870364-11-2

Designed and typeset in Times on Apple Macintosh by Stephen Turner and
Jane Kendall at Common Ground. Printed by Wincanton Print Company in
Somerset on Sylvancoat 100% recycled paper.

The Cover is a detail from a
broadsheet which appeared in
The Independent on
May 1st 1992.
It is available in colour from
Common Ground at £4.50.
Devised by Common Ground.
Typography Peter Wood.
Artwork, Kent & Shaw.
Art Director David Holmes

Contents

Acknowledgements
Common Ground is very grateful to all of the
contributors for their thoughtful and provoca-
tive essays and for helping us in our quest.

This book has been funded by
the Lyndhurst Settlement.
The Conference was subsidised by
The Countryside Commission,
English Heritage and English Nature.
The Local Distinctiveness project has been
supported amongst others by
the Department of the Environment,
the Countryside Commission and
the London Boroughs Grants Committee.

If on arriving at Trude I had not read the city's name written in big letters, I would have thought I was landing at the same airport from which I had taken off. The suburbs they drove me through were no different from the others, with the same little greenish and yellowish houses. Following the same signs we swung round the same flowerbeds in the same square. The downtown streets displayed goods, packages, signs that had not changed at all. This was the first time I had come to Trude, but I already knew the hotel where I happened to be lodged...
Why come to Trude I asked myself. And I already wanted to leave.
'You can resume your flight whenever you like', they said to me, 'but you will arrive at another Trude, absolutely the same, detail by detail. The world is covered by a sole Trude which does not begin and does not end. Only the name of the airport changes'.

Italo Calvino Invisible Cities

A Local Habitation and a Name
Roger Deakin

Local distinctiveness may be described as the sum of the points of connection between the place and the person. It is the things any writer will instinctively smell out and set down. It is a kind of language. It might appear to be an environmental question, but it is quite as much a psychological one.

This collection of papers brings new thought to bear on a problem which has stirred the imagination from Cobbett, through Clare, to Dickens to Morris to Raymond Williams and is the present preoccupation of Common Ground. It is a subject which causes the mind to shift focus dramatically, oscillating from the most abstract to the most particular. My own spontaneous meditation on the subject takes me back eighteen years.

I was sailing with a friend East across the Aegean in a small wooden sloop. We were heading towards the island of Kythnos, but had been blown so far off course by the Meltami that we almost missed it altogether. Having just managed to claw our way around its Southern tip into the shelter of a providential cove, we rode out an anxious night and awoke to rosy-fingered dawn and a perfect beach. There was no soul in sight.

But the beach was not empty. In the shade of a tin shelter on driftwood stilts, occasionally strolling into the sea for a dip and a roll in the shallows, lolled a dozen ample sows. Around mid-morning their owner arrived on a donkey, drew water from a well, and filled the halved-oil-drum troughs.

I have not returned to Kythnos since, but doubt whether such an uncommon thing has survived the Common Agricultural Policy. Where money is scarce, local character is often at its richest and one of the difficulties of thinking about the concept in a relevant, modern way is to address the "margins" as other than merely quaint or eccentric.

Here, at the "margins", the connections between people and place are most evident and easily describable, Here, people are the creators of their worlds rather than users or consumers, and may be accounted the richer for it. In Britain, such values may be felt to be upheld by allotment holders, of whom there were still nearly half a million at the last count, in 1978. Entering an allotment field is like stepping into another part of Europe altogether or South

America. Each plot bears the signature of its owner, and the shared enterprise of improvising a small-scale landscape is a source of endless originality and variety. As places, allotments stand alongside market stalls and local shops in opposition to the supermarket and the new agricutural landscape that is its backdrop. Yet despite the fact that they grow what might be described as inconvenience food, they are, for some reason, popular. They, too, are being squeezed by the pressure of land values.

In terms of this present collection of papers, however, it will be clear that we are not talking about their marginality, but rather the ways in which "margins" go to the heart of the matter. Knowing or getting to know a place is like knowing or loving a person. It is akin to the instinct for monogamy - and it is no coincidence that many place names are also surnames. People's sense of themselves tends to be part of the place where they live or work - "...the blood kinship of the same people living in the same place" (T.S. Eliot, After Strange Gods). To evoke the spirit of such a place is a subtle matter, and subtlety is the key note of many historical attempts to describe the distinctiveness of any particular locality epitomised, perhaps, by Gilbert White's *The Natural History of Selbourne*. And subtlety is certainly the keynote of Ronald Blythe's *Akenfield*, immediately established in his introductory sentences; " It is not a particularly striking place and says little at first meeting". You immediately think of the wonders often encountered in people beyond the reticence of a first meeting. The popularity of *Akenfield*, and more recently of Adam Thorpe's *Ulverton*, is evidence of widespread interest in the question of local distinctiveness. Reading the book, you gradually come to understand the place through the accumulation of detail. Work looms large. Most of Akenfield's inhabitants, at the time of writing in 1969, still worked in the parish. Work connects people with the place. The place, reticent at first, gradually, as Blythe suggests, begins to speak.

What we are talking about is a kind of vernacular which, like all language, is subject to abuse. In "Politics and the English Language" written to protest against the abuse and degradation of the written word, George Orwell felt himself to be open to the same objections as a modern apologist for local distinctiveness:

"Our civilisation is decadent and our language - so the argument runs - must inevitably share in the general collapse. It follows that any struggle against the abuse of language is a sentimental archaism, like preferring candles to electric light or hansom cabs to aeroplanes."

"Sentimental archaism" is, of course, the charge that would appear to lie in wait for any argument against the decline of local distinctiveness. But as Orwell points out, "an effect can become a cause, reinforcing the original cause and producing the same effect in an intensified form, and so on indefinitely. A man may take to drink because he feels himself to be a failure, and then fail all the more completely because he drinks. It is rather the same thing that is happening to the English language. It becomes ugly and inaccurate because our thoughts are foolish, but the slovenliness of our language makes it easier for us to have foolish thoughts."

Resistance is not as Canute-like as it might seem. If the process is reversible for our language, as Orwell believes, could not the same be true of local distinctiveness at the bakery, in the planning office, in the builder's yard, or on the architect's desk? "modern English, especially written English, is full of bad habits which spread by imitation and can be avoided if one takes the necessary trouble."

Architectural vernacular can be thought of as one of the main points of connection between people and place - for its materials constitute its vocabulary. It is subject to all of the perversions that Orwell identifies in relation to English - "Pretentious Diction", "Meaningless Words", "Dying Metaphors". Like any language, it is there to express feelings and ideas, and if they are confused, so will the buildings be. Medieval and Georgian houses and cottages are coherent buildings because they spring from coherent ideas about family life and Home. Domestic architecture now may simply be in as much trouble as family life - hiding behind a facade of old forms for lack of any coherent set of new beliefs.

It was precisely this "humbug", this use of language as an instrument to conceal or prevent thought, instead of for expressing it, that exercised Orwell; "What is above all needed is to let the meaning choose the word and not the other way about." Meaning is something that is experienced from the inside. It has lodged itself in the memory, which , different from recall, becomes part of the person - part, in a sense, of an imaginative process. For appreciation of the essential character of a place is always apprehended in the imagination. The truth of this assertion becomes clearer when the place has been left behind, as in travel, or has gone forever like, say, Food Office orange juice and the British Restaurant just after the war. Most of us who were children then remember the special taste of the orange juice (a treat rivalled only by rosehip syrup) and the special acoustic of the wooden, tin-roofed hut full of collapsible tables and chairs and utility cutlery.

Comprehending, by contrast, happens from the outside. It is possible to comprehend something without it ever being felt or allowed to become part of us. Were the comprehenders - the surveyors, managers, civil servants, governments - to be able to apprehend, they would know that the character of a place bears on all senses at once in mysterious ways. Thus is local distinctiveness one of the touchstones of our being. By giving us access to the past, it offers some hope of access to the present, and to the future - a compass to steer by.

These papers bring different perspectives to a subject which poses fundmental questions about the quality of contemporary life. It is difficult to find a language for these questions which is neither over-simple in its particularity nor over general in its abstraction. We are attempting, 145 years after the publication of *Dombey and Son*, to find a way of addressing the paradoxes and contradictions which Dickens captured so forcefully and ironically in his description of the destruction of the old Camden Town by the new railway system - "that indomitable monster, Death!":

"In short, the yet unfinished and unopened Railroad was in progress; and, from the very core of all this dire disorder, trailed smoothly away, upon its mighty course of civilization and improvement."

The coming of the new Railroad to Camden Town.

Staggs's Gardens was uncommonly incredulous. It was a little row of houses, with little squalid patches of ground before them, fenced off with old doors, barrel staves, scraps of tarpaulin, and dead bushes; with bottomless tin kettles and exhausted iron fenders, thrust into the gaps. Here, the Staggs's Gardeners trained scarlet beans, kept fowls and rabbits, erected rotten summer-houses (one was an old boat), dried clothes, and smoked pipes. Some were of opinion that Staggs's Gardens derived its name from a deceased capitalist, one Mr Staggs, who had built it for his delectation. Others, who had a natural taste for the country, held that it dated from those rural times when the antlered herd, under the familiar denomination of Staggses, had resorted to its shady precincts. Be this as it may, Staggs's Gardens was regarded by its population as a sacred grove not to be withered by Railroads; and so confident were they generally of its long outliving any such ridiculous inventions, that the master chimney-sweeper at the corner, who was understood to take the lead in the local politics of the Gardens, had publicly declared that on the occasion of the Railroad opening, if it ever did open, two of his boys should ascend the flues of his dwelling, with instructions to hail the failure with derisive cheers from the chimney pots.

Charles Dickens *Dombey and Son.*

Losing Your Place

Sue Clifford and Angela King

The main players fall silent, the filming is over, the recording is finished, but the sound technician has hushed everyone to get some 'atmos'. Coughs, car noise echoing off the warehouses, birdsong, boards creaking, trees breathing in the wind, these are the sounds of the everyday, so particular to this place, that to cut the film and add studio voiceovers needs an underlay of this local atmosphere in order to ensure continuity and authenticity.

That elusive particularity, so often undervalued as 'background noise', is as important as the stars. It is the richness we take for granted.

How do we know where we are in time and space? How do we understand ourselves in the world?

Common Ground has been exploring and developing a new concept, that of local distinctiveness. It is characterised by elusiveness, it is instantly recognizable yet difficult to describe. It is simple yet may have profound meaning to us. It demands a poetic quest and points up the shortcomings in all those attempts to understand the things around us by compartmentalising them, fragmenting, quantifying, reducing.

Local distinctiveness is essentially about places and our relationship with them. It is as much about the commonplace as about the rare, about the everyday as much as the endangered, and about the ordinary as much as the spectacular. In other cultures it might be about people's deep relationship with the land. Here discontinuities have left us with vestiges of appreciation but few ways of expressing the power which places can have over us. But many of us have strong allegiances to places, complex and compound appreciation of them, and we recognize that nature, identity and place have strong bonds.

We sometimes forget that ours is a cultural landscape. It is our great creation: underpinned by nature, it is a physical thing and an invisible web. It is held together by stonewalls and subsidies, ragas and Northumbrian pipes, Wensleydale sheep and halal butchers, whiskies of Islay and Fenland skies, bungalows and synagogues, pubs and the Padstow Obby' Oss, round barrows and rapping, high streets and Ham stone, laver bread and Devon lanes, door details and dialect.

Places are process and story as well as artefact, layer upon layer of our continuing history and nature's history intertwined. Places offer an exposition of their evolution, given sensitive development and barefoot education, everyplace is its own living museum, dynamic and filled with sensibilities to its own small richnesses. These are places we know when we are in them. Meaning is entrapped in the experience of change, symbolisms and significance cling to seemingly ordinary buildings, trees, artefacts. Particularity based in nature on the foundations of geology and climate, has diverged with the alchemy of life, the articulation of the social and economic demands of successive societies, the narratives of myth and legend, and the ethical and cultural variations over the time. Places are different from each other.

We have long recognized the importance of diversity. Most travel guides, geology books, volumes on architecture and language begin by asserting how varied our land and people are. Yet we have been party to a massive burst of homogenisation, some of it in the name of conservation, which is bleaching the richness from our lives.

The variegation which we and nature have created in sharing our development seems to appeal to our eye for richness. We may scientise our interest in bio-diversity, offer critical appraisal of stark geometric buildings, intellectualise arguments about differentiation being 'a good thing', but the truth is that we revel in detail. Subtlety and complication, flavours which are not immediately apparent please our palate/palette.

We are able to pick out a face in football crowd, see a tiny yellow bird high up in a tree of a hundred thousand leaves, we can place a wine by its taste and sneeze at things we cannot even smell, we have acute faculties which enjoy the challenges of complexity. We often know and feel things for which words cannot be found, despite having one of the richest languages in the world. We are emotional, subjective beings, with memories and with interests in the future, as well as the here and now. We are provoked to reverie by the smallest of things.

How then has it happened that we can stand in many high streets, factories, fields or forests and feel we could be anywhere? Why does MacDonald's force upon our high streets an idea born in corporate strategy meetings thousands of miles away? Why do we have huge brown signs from motorways telling us where to find Robin Hood Country and the White Cliffs Experience? Why are we planting the same trees everywhere? Why are only mountains 'beautiful' landscapes, and big and old buildings worthy of care and attention? Why does the pursuit of standards now result in standardisation. Apples, bricks, sheep and gates, all of which have had generations of careful guided evolution creating qualities related to conditions of locality and need, no longer show the differentiation which whispers rather than shouts where you are.

Partial comprehension of loss has begun to force meaningless, token choices upon us. We are offered a Chiltern or a Mayfair or a Wensleydale house on the same housing estate or in Devon, Nottinghamshire or Cleveland. Difference for difference sake with no reflection, no interest in craftsmanship, appropriateness or locality, debases all that has gone before, and pays no homage to the extraordinary potential latent in the achievements of our time. Anyway they are all made out of red brick (from the same brick company) with hardwood windows (from the same rainforest) with the same front doors and the streets have the same paving and kerb stones, the curves and cul de sacs mirror each other, the gardens have the same cypresses and whatever the garden centres are selling this year.

While homogenising forces have been at work so have enriching ones. Our culture, or cultures have hardly ever been static. In our context a dynamic culture has been a permeable culture, an open work. The many peoples who have settled in Britain over the ages, and in the last few decades, have brought ideas, foods, music, festivals, languages, cultural differentiation which far from diluting the already rich mix has added new dynamism, and new layers of particularity to different places.

Dilution has come through closed minds, aggressive assertion of national and corporate identity, blind searching for the single perfect barley strain, the imposition of ideas exported or imported without reflection (in the architectural context, the exchange of ideas need never have resulted in a single style of buildings across the world, lacking any referential humility to place, climate and culture).

The suppression of the Gaelic and Welsh languages must be a loss to us all. In Welsh there are at least 40 words for rain, one example of the differentiation of the common place, which comes from generations of close dialogue with nature.

BBC English has a lot to answer for. Bill Bryson has said about the language 'if we should be worrying about anything to do with the future of English, it should be not that the various strands will drift apart, but that they will grow indistinguishable'. He reminds us that 'English... has been... immeasurably enriched by the successive linguistic waves that washed over the British Isles. But it is closer to the truth to say that the language we speak today is rich and expressive not so much because new words were imposed upon it as because they were welcomed'.

This latter sentiment offers a way forward.

Welcoming rather than imposition demands working together. Recognizing there is a need to reinforce the qualitative aspects of our everyday lives, Common Ground has been working to offer people ideas, information and inspiration to affect change for the better in their own localities. The work on local distinctiveness aspires to arousing diverse community based actions, as well as creative and responsive policy making and practice in voluntary organisations, local and national institutions and local authorities and the corporate sector too.

To offer formulae would be to deny the basic philosophy that we are expressing. Provocations, examples and questions are helpful, we assert that local formulation is always necessary, and that much is to be learnt from exploration with local people. There are many ways in. The creation of an ABC of your own locality is an exercise which brings together all manner of things ordered only by their name, strange juxtapositions jolt complacency. Everything begins with equal status in the gathering, out of which discussion can emerge over what is important to whom, why, when and where.

Local distinctiveness can encompass so many things and affects everyone. In exploring the idea Common Ground has found it useful to work around key words, which allow reinterpretation for every different circumstance: detail, particularity, patina, authenticity. We are talking of quality in the everyday. Because these things are not straightforward or easy to pigeonhole, often involve emotional attachment and are hard to communicate they are treated as 'soft' by the media. Because they are impossible to put a money value on or to explain through equations, these unquantifiable 'intangibles' are likely to be marginalised by the professionals. Debate rages, and decisions are taken which often leave out the very things that make life worth living.

Brody in describing the decision making culture of the Athapaskan hunter captures the spirit of what we are trying to say : ' To disconnect the variables, to compartmentalise the thinking, is to fail to acknowledge its sophistication and completeness....To make a good, wise, sensible...choice is to accept the interconnection of all possible factors, and avoids the mistake of seeking rationally to focus on any one consideration that is held as primary. What is more, the decision is taken in the doing : there is no step or pause between theory and practice.'

Closer to our world, scientists of many disciplines engaged in the fascinating unveiling of ideas around Chaos theory are moving away from reductionism towards looking at the whole and are acknowledging that the objective and subjective are less clear cut. Ideas of scaling form an important part of their revelations.

Local
Scale is important, as is the question of who defines it. We are talking of a fineness of grain - the neighbourhood, the locality, the parish, the housing estate, the high street, the village, the suburb, perhaps even the street as defined by those who live and work and play there. The area to which people feel they belong, and which belongs to them through familiarity, or which they have chosen and are claiming anew.

It is not regional diversity but *local distinctiveness*. The bigger the scale the more reduced the sensitivity and the easier it becomes to steamroller strategies for the 'greater good' which prescribe the same solutions to subtley different circumstances encouraging convergence and homogeneity....thereby missing the whole point.

When we change scale we think and behave differently: nations are abstractions, regions are generally defined from the outside in, they are about form and function, they are academic, institutional or political creations.

Locality needs to be defined from the inside, with a cultural and natural base, less abstraction, more detail.

Attempts should not be made to reduce local distinctiveness to an essence. It is a compound thing and a messy one as well as being dynamic hence its elusiveness. It cannot be summarised. It may be variegated within, but have a unity and integrity in the mingling of its parts. Smallness should not be confused with simplicity.

Returning to the Chaos theorists, Mandelbrot asked 'How long is the coast of Britain?' (following LF Richardson). It seems so simple, but he recognized and asserted that any answer would be dependent upon the distance from which one was taking the measurement. Someone measuring a satellite map would give a much smaller figure than someone walking every inlet, and for a snail every pebble would add to the length. It is dependent upon the scale at which one sets the dividers/ruler to work. In other words it all depends.

While we have made the world smaller with aeroplanes and trains and cars, travellators and elevators, we still have to pace most of our activities to our size and to our own walking. It is at this scale and speed that we see and savour most. At the greater scales we can understand patterns in a different way, but to act at this level risks inattention to people and the quotidian. Substitution of abstract words begins to desensitise - the public for people, sites for streets or fields, environment for places, natural resources for woods and clear streams: abstractions which disengage us from reality, and give professionals a mandate to act without care for the detail.

Distinctiveness

Distinctiveness is not the same as diversity, for it involves much more than variety, it degrades them to be used interchangeably. It is not about difference for its own sake, but recognizes that heterogeneity suggests richness: historical, cultural and ecological. Diversity is but one dimension. Current ecological preoccupations about biodiversity brings it to the fore. But biodiversity has a restricted range of usefulness, offering little help in argument for the tundra and so often the cultural is left out. The proliferation of varieties within species which have resulted from hundreds, possibly thousands of years of selection in horticulture and agriculture are often not considered.

Local distinctiveness links meaning, identity, patina and authenticity. Meaning implies many associations, deep significance and is sensed in the power of the place. Identity is bound up with affection for everyday activities and the symbolism of features and festivals.

Rarely do strict edges exist, as at the coast or because the army is using the land, or the green belt actually works or through dramatic quality of changing geology or geomorphology. Gradation is the common way in which one place ends and another begins.

Where two habitats meet the ecotone exhibits a richness of intermingling of species, often richer than the pure habitats it buffers. Just as in town some streets are dominated by small Indian shops and others by big chain stores, the area of greatest fascination may well be where they overlap.

Just as geologists are excited by unconformity, so archaeologists tell the time by reading the overlaps - a line of a Roman road cutting across field systems implies they are older, planners work with zones and designations. But we must not get diverted in looking for and drawing boundaries. Our preoccupation must be with the idea of local distinctiveness as experienced by people.

We should not from the outside be drawing contours of similarity and somewhere away from the epicentre saying this is a different place. The definitions should be from the inside out and admit of variegation: it is possible for things to be compatible and very different and yet part of the same place... the buildings there may be a 'confliction' of styles and materials but together they make the place special.

Detail
In Australia vast areas seem to us to look the same, but the seasoned eye and the cultured brain sees and describes minute detail, water can be found from the smallest/subtlest constellation of clues, stories cling to small marks on rocks and the slightest rise can be a landmark for miles.

We seem to have a much greater capacity to see than we have to describe. Hence people sense when something has gone from their local scene, but can't articulate it... it could be a change in paving stones or the loss of a tree, it could be changes in the air quality resulting in the loss of moss growth and irridescence at certain times of year, it could be the displacement of a family firm by a chain store in its universal livery. And we tend to see things altogether, the fruit salad seems less good if someone has picked out all the banana.

Detail is important in our lives. Whatever our work or pleasure, our attention and affections are held by small complications, intricacies and provocations. We thrive on gossip, TV soaps, brick not concrete, things which repeat with endless variations at different scales, we were influenced by fractals long before someone gave them a name.

Just as Thomas Hardy talks of divining a mountain in the dark by the absence of stars, we recognize where we are through many different kinds of 'cues', and often we sense what is there through something else.

Ecologists use the term indicator species. Dog's Mercury suggests there was ancient woodland here. Geologists (following aboriginal practice) recognize the presence of certain minerals by the plants growing in those parts, sand wort is known as leadwort in Derbyshire, Lancashire and Cheshire. Pollution and lichen experts read the presence of sulphur dioxide in the absence of Lobaria pulmonaria. We can 'see' the salt line along roadsides in the centre of England by the presence of coastal plants such as sea spurrey. A Warwickshire gate lets us know subliminally we are in that county not in Gloucestershire.

Original attempts to map climate had to rely upon patterns read from vegetation, forests and deserts echoing particular limiting factors. Only when wind and temperature could be monitored by scattered weather stations and at altitude did scientists find affirming evidence of coincidence through direct information. The invisible had been understood through the visible. The effects of Chernobyl's deathly clouds can still be traced on Cumbrian hills through sheep with blue marks.

History is often pieced together by detective work from traces and footprints. The interesting distribution of the Mazzard cherries along the Tamar valley and in one or two places in North Devon has lead people to speculate that they were brought in by the Huguenots, they add particularity and harbour secrets.

There are many latent languages which we decipher without realizing what richness we perceive. There is much non verbal communication between us and a place we know well. As well as responding to the obvious, we identify signs, hints, clues, traces, suggestions, gestures, intimations, and they gather further richness through juxtaposition. We respond to mosaic. We need the nourishment of detail, in things as ordinary as rumples in a field, detail in doors and windows, dialect, local festival days, seasonal variation in the goods on sale in the market, to subtly stimulate our senses and sensibilities.

What is there in a Cornish hedge
The broken herring bone pattern of stones,
The gorse, the ragged rick,
The way the little elms are,
Sea-bent, sea-shorn
That so affects the heart?

(AL Rowse, Cornish Landscape)

Authenticity
The real and the genuine hold a strength of meaning for us. If the advertising world is to be believed this is worth, and costs, a lot: 'It's the real thing', Levi 501s, Champagne.

Wensleydale cheese: why is it important to makers and gourmets that this cheese continues to be made in this valley and not the next? Amongst the reasons to do with the need for jobs, comes also an understanding that cows of this place, eating grass in this valley, with expertise built here over generations combine to create a food which is particular, authentic and good. Its making brings dignity and pride to the place, since the people who make it are experts, the people who grow the grass to feed the cows are implicated in this. The relationships breed culture and identity which has meaning for the people who live and work here and for those who chance upon it or make it their destination. The landscape that is created and sustained by this activity is one in which mixed grass, wild flowers, barns have a real role and sustain a landscape plotted and pieced with interrelationships.

If the discussion was about Gevrey Chambertin, Julienas and Fleurie, the initiates would nod knowingly about the discrete charms of the different slopes, soils, sun and seasons: the French have made a profession out of the particular. Appelation controllée carries important kudos, identity, place and quality are intimately bound together. The place of origin, the knowledge of derivation is real and important. People can tell the difference. If trace elements can make the difference between life and death, they can certainly make the difference between good and better, and the educated nose can tell. Recent EC regulations are currently calling for protective registration of Geographical Indications and Designations of Origin.

SJ Gould draws a neat analysis of authenticity of object, use and place. He deliberates over the lack of interest we show in a fibreglass dinosaur as opposed to the real fossils, the San Francisco tram full of tourists at noon rather than the workers in the early morning, and the lack of inspiration to be gained from seeing London Bridge somewhere in the USA.

To see a Somerset hedge laid in a Midland pattern, to hear theatrical Yorkshire accents tracing the words of DH Lawrence, to taste a Bakewell pudding made without almonds.......Authenticity and integrity are related. We use words such as pastiche, facade, kitsch, ersatz, Disney to denegrate forcibly. Much criticism of the packaging of history as 'Heritage', has followed the degrading of cultural complexity to marketing one liners - Bronte Country, 1066 Country or 'Coventry: the City where legends are made'.

It should be perfectly possible to reinforce the medievalness of York, the Thomas Hardy connections in Dorset, but so often you are left with a stage set, a marketing idea of a 'tourist destination', a kind of deadness, one dimensional and unsatisfying. If we leave no room for peeling paint, time before and since, access to the life of the place now, we present a picture which is dishonest and unreal. Local distinctiveness is not necessarily about beauty, but it must be about truth.

Particularity

The unusual, the special, the strange, the idiosyncratic, the rare may be important factors in giving a place its sense of itself, but the matrix exerts the binding force. The commonplace defines identity: the locally abundant plants, the specific wall building methods, the precise ingredients for recipes. In one Derbyshire town doctors apparently scribble NFI on many of their patients' notes decipherable to them as Normal for Ilkeston.

Georgian houses great and small have a recognizable similarity of form, function and facade, based upon proportional rules. Their differences are in their social declaration (first rate, second rate and third rate houses of Bloomsbury), their tasks (workers houses in Barnsbury, the 10th Earl of Moray's estate in Edinburgh's New Town), their materials (yellow oolitic limestone of Bath, red brick of Nottinghamshire), their relations to the land and each other. So despite the homogenising potential, they serve as wonderful example of richness.

The point here is not to be preoccupied by difference, but by appropriateness to and expressiveness of time and place. While all leaves are doing the same basic job they have developed drip tips, hairs, etc. to accomodate to local conditions, all species produce different kinds of leaves, and every leaf on the same tree is different, the rules dictated by photosynthesis and family do not sacrifice individuation.

Patina

Age has to be recognised as having been gathered, hence the paradoxical vitality of patina.

Go to Dorset, compare a deep ploughed field of a hundred acres with an area of ten tenacre fields. Read the richness in the latter perhaps neolithic strip lynchetts or medieval ridge and furrow with overlays of Enclosure hedgerows, never ploughed or strewn with herbicide or fertilizer, clear winterbournes and watercress beds: rich in history and natural history. Or go to the East End of London and compare a sixties, seventies or eighties estate with the Huguenot buildings, bagel shops, a mosque in an old synagogue and the tandoori restaurants of Brick Lane.

The crude sacrifices made by large scale and rapid change demean us. The remnants of the accumulation of activity, the layers or fragments of which can be experienced or read, can be added to without recourse to brutalism. Dynamism and vitality should be great allies for local distinctiveness. Attempts to arrest both progress and decay in a Cotswold village, or the cultural melée of Brick Lane, brings danger of reducing the richness and fermentation to leave a frozen moment, the real place and people having sunk below the waves of preciousness or poverty.

Local distinctiveness must be about history continuing through the present (not about the past) and it is about creating the future. There is a great difference in people simply dressing up in Victorian clothes and a festival such as Carnival which builds on gutsy traditions carried forth and back and changed to new circumstances.

Local distinctiveness is about *not* separating out the many views and many factors, but recognising their synergism. Questions should seek ever greater detail and ever ramifying connections. Yet so many decisions are made based on one dimensional argument or recognizing patterns which are then over simplified, abstracted and turned into strategies and policy statements which could be about anyplace, and will inevitably lead to the building of virtually the same village hall in a corner of Kent or Cumberland, or bypasses through fields and woods with meaning to the locality, building a stile or a seat from a national pattern book, ordering paving and railings which Carlisle, Camden or Christchurch might have, designing carparks for anywhere. It is salutary to recall that utopia means nowhere...the philosophising which builds the ideal usually imagines nothing has been there before, and that life and culture will evolve no further.

Questing for local distinctiveness must err towards the inclusive and welcoming, it is not about designating areas more beautiful or more derelict or worthy of grants. It is about working on an idea that anyone can use to demonstrate the valuables of their place to anyone else. It is about accepting that places mean more to us than we are able to say, and beginning to talk more to each other at the local level about demanding the best of the new.

It is crucial that knowledge, new ideas and wisdom are shared. The tumbleweed expertise of the professional learnt and practised all over the place, the migrant with new cultural eyes, the indigene with generations of often undervalued place-based wisdom, all have different richnesses of perception to offer.

This implies a radical shift in the way in which we plan and prognosticate... towards more responsive, detailed, fractioned way of changing things. There never has been any need to bulldoze the whole building site, or to demand the pronunciation of your 'h's.

Common Ground

The forces of homogenisation rob us of visible and invisible things which have meaning to us, they devalue our longitudinal wisdom and erase the fragments from which to piece together the stories of nature and history through which our humanity is fed. They stunt our sensibilities and starve our imagination.

And as Bachelard has said 'imagination separates us from the past as well as reality, it faces the future. If we cannot imagine, we cannot foresee'. Our interest in local distinctiveness is a profound concern for our common future.

References
Gaston Bachelard *The Poetics of Space* Beacon Books 1958/69
Hugh Brody *Maps and Dreams* Faber and Faber 1981/86
Bill Bryson *Mother Tongue* Penguin 1990
Stephen J Gould *Eight Little Piggies* Jonathan Cape 1993
Benoit Mandelbrot *The Fractal Geometry of Nature* Freeman 1977

Some Welsh words for rain.

bwrw *to* rain	*byrlymu* pouring very quickly
glawio raining	*llifo* flooding
bwrwglaw raining	*towlud* (dial.)throwing
dafnu spotting	*taflu* throwing
pigo spotting	*hegar law* fierce rain
glaw mân drizzle	*lluwchlaw* sheets of rain
gwlithlaw drizzle	*chwipio bwrw* whiplash rain
brasfwrw big spaced drops	*pistyllio* fountain rain
sgrympian (dial.) short sharp shower	*piso* pissing down
cawodi showering	*curlaw* beating rain
arllwys pouring	*tywallt* absolutely bucketing
tollti pouring	*stido*(dial.) thrashing down
dymchwel pulling down	*tresio* maximum intensity
Mae hi'n bwrw hen wragedd a ffyn	It's raining old women and sticks!

Please bear in mind that I have been away from home, for almost twenty five years, and, as a result, the list might lack comprehensiveness. Further, whilst most words listed occur in 'RP' Welsh, some are dialectical forms which are probably peculiar to the locality of my birthplace, the village of Beddgelert, and may not be familiar to the men (and women) of Dyfed.

John Christopher Williams, personal correspondence, 1989.

Nature and Change:
the two faces of naturalisation

Richard Mabey

Our sense of locality, I suspect, is rooted as deeply in territorial feelings as in topography. We become imprinted by places, and familiar with them just as a cat or fox does. We plod out private routes, touch trees, and mark (in our imaginations, at least) our special spots - a bend in a road, a gate to lean on, a face glimpsed in a trunk. Loyalty to these marking posts can be fierce and personal, and given without the slightest regard for what is locally distinctive.

Certainly the first place that I got to know and love when I was growing up as a rather gipsyish boy in the Chilterns, didn't have a trace of local identity. It was the remains of a country estate at the back of our road. The big house had been demolished in the 20s, the landscaped grounds were reverting to wilderness, and all us neighbourhood kids (and a good many adults, too) treated it as the local common. We stalked it like aborigines, marking out a cryptic network of landmarks, totems, forbidden zones and hideouts; but its random mix of brick piles, bramble patches and parkland cedar trees could have been anywhere from Surrey to Galloway. What was important - and distinctive - to us were the meanings we had given them.

It was not until my late teens that I recognised, with something of a shock, that places could also have an objective character. I was on a first trip to the Norfolk coast (which proved to have its own tangy sense of place - but that is another story), and on the way passed through that vast and mysterious inland sand-bowl called the Breckland. The sandstorms and great bustards had vanished long before, but not the bizarre wind-breaks that had been created in the 18th century from lopped and layered Scots pines. These stunted trees rising from the sandy fields beyond the sinister US bomber base at Lakenheath, were like no other landscape I had seen. It was a desert, an English badlands.

These pine-belts still give me gooseflesh when I am driving east, and I am pleased that they now have official recognition as a unique and defining element of the Breckland scene. But what also strikes me is what ironic and incongruous features they are for such a role. They are, for a start, a more or less alien tree which hasn't grown naturally in eastern England for 6000 years. They also played a crucial part in the process of parliamentary enclosure in East Anglia, which helped to drive indigenous commoners off the land, and helped obliterate the open heaths and mobile sand that had been a previous era's contribution to Breckland's local distinctiveness.

The latest irony is that more than a century later in the 1920s, Breckland became the site of one of the largest and earliest Forestry Commission plantations. Scots and various other kinds of pine, were again planted out in rows in the sand, but this time in vast, dour blankets that were to become a symbol of the homogenisation of the countryside, of a process that was making immense tracts of Britain from Inverness to Norfolk indistinguishable.

The contribution of nature to local character is often like this, ambivalent, mutable, as likely to be some new, accommodating growth that fits the rhythms and continuity of the place as an ancient presence or heritage cliché. My home town of Berkhamsted is probably named after the birch trees that grow on the acid plateau above the settlement. They still thrive there, but despite a rather better understanding of landscape history than I had as a schoolboy pagan, I simply cannot think of my home country as "the place of the birches". If the trees do figure in my sense of my own patch, they have become an unconscious backcloth, a kind of second nature yet to be put to the loyalty test.

Natural features were often obvious or important enough to provide names for places, but the names usually outlive them. There are no lime trees left in Linwood or Lyndhurst in the New Forest. The ravens have long gone from Ravensden on the outskirts of industrial Bedford. And despite the annual neo-Celtic festival in Glastonbury, I doubt that woad is any longer a significant local crop (glasto - is woad in Old Celt). Even when naming features survive, they can seem as remote and cryptic as Latin family mottos on village war memorials. The weed fat-hen is still common enough amongst the sugar beet fields of mid-Suffolk. It was called melde in Old English, eaten as an important staple vegetable in prehistoric and even medieval East Anglia, and probably gave its name to the village of Milden, near Sudbury. A few present-day inhabitants certainly believed so, and about fifteen years ago, put up a cast-iron statue of the weed on the edge of the village. It is one of the most bizarre and distinctive parish boundary signs in the country, but I wonder what most of the rest of this still predominantly farming community make of it, having spent the last few centuries trying to wipe out plants like this from the fields?

Features as arcane as this are just too bookish or ghostly to contribute to a real sense of locality. Yet those that are striking and persistent can transcend our personal territorial symbols, and become communal motifs, sources of pride and maybe even passion, something which can join locals and outsiders in a common sense of place. The wild daffodils that have given the country between Dymock and Ledbury the nickname of the Golden Triangle, are a good example. A few centuries ago many parts of Britain could have offered the sight of whole copses and meadows lapped with yellow under the March sunshine. Now, it is only a few oases like this stretch of the border country that have the plant in any quantities. It was already becoming a speciality of this region in the 1930s, when the Great Western Railway used to run 'Daffodil Specials' here, and local farmers and fruit growers threw open their fields to pickers. After the last war, the local colonies were reduced still further by agricultural changes, and local daffodil consciousness declined. But there are signs it is picking up again. There are local daffodil festivals, and a remarkable cooperative effort by landowners, local authorities, local people, has created a ten mile walk through local woods, meadows, churchyards that is never out of the sight of the "golden host".

Similarly, limestone in the Yorkshire Dales is recognised by native and tourist alike as one of the defining features of the place. It isn't quite like limestone anywhere else in Britain, in Derbyshire or the Mendips or the Brecon Beacons, say. The difference is not just a matter of natural geological features, of limestone pavements and scree slopes, but of what local people have done with the stone: the way drystone walling follows the patterns of layering in the bare terraces, the "found-stones" and vernacular gargoyles that adorn so many cottage walls and roofs.

This is a landscape where the human presence has been sympathetic towards local quirks and savours. These days most human manipulation of natural features involves a deliberate ironing-out of local identity and diversity for the sake of commercial convenience. Forestry plantations, CAP cash crop fields, new golf courses, are as characterless as international airports. Off-the-peg ornamental trees - Japanese double flowering cherries, robinias, black alders - are giving a uniform, garden festival look to towns across the land, that maybe once sported indigenous willows and whitebeams. Even conservation policies, with the very best of intentions, can lead to a levelling out. Britain's wonderfully diverse legacy of hedges, for instance, are declining and disappearing, and it is good that there are government backed schemes to regenerate them. But the revival of interest in hedgerows has been accompanied by a rather indiscriminate zeal for management for its own sake, and tall Exmoor beech windbreaks, Suffolk ancient wood remnants and thick Dorset double-rows, are all being beaten down to the level and scale of Midland quicksets.

But maybe I am being a killjoy. Isn't a regimented living hedge better than a vanished local speciality? Aren't street robinias brighter and more resilient than pollarded willows? Mightn't a commitment to local distinctiveness be difficult to disentangle from high-handed puritanism, or isolation, or even an unpleasant xenophobia (as in the recent pogrom against American ruddy ducks)? Earlier this year I was driving back from Shropshire on the first warm day of March, and all the way through the Long Mynd hills pairs of buzzards - tourists' eagles - were spiralling in courtship displays on the thermals. As soon as I was down on the Midland plain, they were gone. I marvelled at what an extraordinary thing the buzzard line is, stretching as it does from Dorset through the Cotswolds and the eastern Lakes, even dividing lowland Scotland in two; and how entering buzzard country, and seeing those meditative, soaring shapes above the hills, is a sure sign of having crossed into the west. Then I remembered that this is an entirely unnatural state for the bird, which a century and half ago, before persecution by the game lobby, had been common throughout Britain. Its current distribution, as flavoursome a westerly thing as cider or chapels, is, like that of the wild daffodil, an indication of unnatural depletion as much as local distinctiveness.

And as Dutch disease got a grip again this spring, I thought too about the elms, whose story is another salutary if ambivalent parable. Elms are one of the most locally diverse of all our native trees. Different types, reproducing largely by suckers, have evolved in different parts of Britain: stiff, fastigiate kinds, twiggy kinds, varieties with an almost black bark, an almost infinite variety of leaf shapes to match, and some, like the Boxworth elm of the country round Huntingdon, more or less resistant to the disease. The great elm specialist, Professor R.H. Richens, found that there was a distinctive elm type in almost every East Anglian valley. The local trees, isolated genetically from those in the next valley, were the source of the cuttings and suckers used to make the local hedges, which after a while formed a treescape subtly different from that in the next village. Ironically, the human inhabitants were probably quite unaware of these botanical differences; and though the genetic variety of the nation's elms is part of the species insurance policy, the cloning of local varieties means that if any one tree in a village catches the disease they will likely all go under. Local distinctivness in terms of natural resources, pursued too narrowly, can represent a dead end, a state of siege as much as an oasis.

The fenlands of East Anglia are an extreme example of a distinctive locality which has become an impoverished landscape for all its life forms. It is still a place with a powerful aura, determined by the huge imperatives of sky, wind and water. Yet most of its old liveliness has been drained and sprayed into oblivion, and it has become a place of sad paradoxes. I have seen scores of black-dressed women hunched over the potato crop like a vision of the worst times of the 19th century agricultural depression. And a few hundred yards away, signs warning passersby to stay off the fields because of the 'deadly poisons'.

People living on the edge of the Fens have an inexhaustible supply of slanderous stories about the inhabitants of this drained swamp. They are, the myths go, insular, inbred and violent - 'Fen Tigers'. They use their children as slave labour in the fields. The Fens are eastern England's Balkans, and every stereotype that has been glimpsed or fabricated about the rural population at large has been magnified and dumped on this vast plain of fertile peat. Even the landscape itself - featureless flat rectangles clear to the horizon - can seem like a bleak caricature of the modern farmscape.

The unusual thing is that the local people themselves don't dispute many of these images. They are acutely aware of the brutalising effects of centuries of isolation, of the ceaseless battle against flooding, and of the corrosive influence of modern agriculture. In the 19th century rheumatism and 'the ague' were endemic, and opium use was common right up until the 1920s. Today it is depression and drink, and 'fen syndrome', described by psychiatrists as a kind of 'cultural retardation', is a matter of medical record in the region.

But people have loved and still love this place. The poet John Clare did, even after the first stages of its enforced enclosure and modernisation had helped drive him mad. Edward Storey loves it today, and reading his poems one can catch something of fenland's melancholy, harrowing beauty. It is a measure of just how vital locality is to us that we cling to, and can get comfort from, the slightest shadows and echoes of the old spirit of a place.

***

Are there any answers to these conundrums? Any way of maintaining distinctive local characteristics that are palpable to both insiders and outsiders, without the damaging effects of isolation, introversion and withdrawal? Perhaps since nature is a metaphor for, as well as a real contributor to, local distinctiveness, it wouldn't be out of place to look briefly at the way in which ecologists explore and account for the changes in isolated communities. It is a branch of the science known as 'island biogeography', and I think its findings are significant in many ways to how we think about local distintiveness.

Isolation can be both a driving force and a barrier to evolution. The different species and races of finches that had evolved on the islands of the Galapagos group were one of the clues that led Darwin to the theory of evolution. But populations of creatures that are cut off from the outside world are also vulnerable, and can fall prey to inbreeding, disease and natural catastrophe. Unless an island ecosystem is regularly replenished by new species or varieties from outside, it can become slowly but progressively degraded. When the volcanic island of Krakatau erupted in 1883, all traces of life were destroyed. But within a year, lizards and crabs were being washed in by the tides, and minute spiders, fungus spores and seeds - all alien invaders were coming in on the wind from every part of Indonesia. Today the remnant island of Rakata is covered by young Asian rain forest.

Most of Britain - indeed much of the earth's surface - is now in the condition, ecologically speaking, of a fragmented collection of islands. Wetlands are starved of water, woods cut off from each other by cutlivated land. They are vulnerable to exactly the same kinds of degenerative changes to which real islands are prone.

Think for a moment of one of the most characteristic features of many rural parishes, the local wood, these days probably surrounded by arable. The worst things that can happen to it, in ascending order of awfullness, are probably being barricaded off as a kind of ecological isolation ward; being allowed slowly to become impoverished; or being swamped by well-meaning alien plantings. In the same way the worst fates for a whole community may be fossilisation as a heritage area; dying of anachronism; or being entirely repopulated by outsiders and outside ways.

Is there any alternative way, in which places and communities can be given transfusions of new life from the outside without compromising their distinctiveness or making their inhabitants feel oppressed and 'colonised'? The touchstone may be whether the new is naturalised or imposed. Imposition we are all too familiar with. It is the rape field grown for subsidy, the international style filling station, the commemorative Japanese maple.

Naturalisation on the other hand, in both the human and natural worlds, involves the slow absorption of a newcomer, which becomes part of the host community without abandoning its essential identity. It also suggests, I think, a certain fittingness, something which goes with the grain and texture of what is already there. It is Thames valley gravel pits and buddleia on building sites. One of the most fascinating examples of this in modern England has been the colonising of the River Don in Sheffield by feral fig trees. They are not only striking to look at, but stuck amongst the decaying steelworks have a poignant sense of history and place about them. Their story is a remarkable one of harmonious naturalisation. It seems as if they grew from seeds carried downstream in human sewage (and maybe in waste from food factories), and have the steel industry to thank for their successful establishment in the 1920s. River water was used for cooling purposes in the factories, and the outfall kept the water in the river at a steady temperature of 20 degrees C - warm enough to germinate those seeds of this Mediterranean species when they fetched up on muddy shores. But when stricter controls were introduced on effluent quality, and, later, local steel manufacture went into decline, the river's temperature returned to normal and no new trees were able to sprout.

Local people have become proud of these trees, and have fought successfully to save many of them in the face of tidy-minded officials and developers. As one has said, "they are as much a part of Sheffield's history as the old steam-hammers and Bessemer converters" - a strange but heartening destiny for a species that began its journey, as did the first neolithic settlers and landscape-shapers of our islands, in the eastern Mediterranean.

Local Distinctiveness:
an architectural conundrum
Gillian Darley

To be distinctive is to leave an imprint, in the mind or on the eye. What are we discussing? A recognisable or familiar quality; one that can be captured, taught or copied? Is local distinctiveness just a trace on the palate of a good flavour or is it a commodity, to be bottled and hard sold?

Summoning up an exact picture of a place, imprinting an architectural image in one's mind, is like the small child's drawing of a house. Very literal and very certain, it is also highly misleading - pitched roof, chimney, front door and windows.

W. H. Hudson was born in 1841 and lived in Argentina until he was 28. Arriving in England he travelled extensively, to places with historic and picturesque associations - Silchester, Stonehenge, Wells or the Otter Valley - publishing 'Afoot in England' in 1909.

He warned against the second impression of any lovely scene, likely to be a poor version of the first -"the mental image must always be better than its reality." There were many places he would never revisit for fear of disillusionment. A wise, if abrupt, decision in a traveller, it is no way to consider the chimera of place.

Hudson's self-protection against the quirks of memory and the tug of the emotions is both of his time and ours. He was indulgent to his sentiments, while our protection against the failure of memory - or perhaps just misunderstanding - is to charge on, making it up as we go along.

The architectural problem concerns a fundamental misunderstanding. Backward somersaults are always difficult, and generally fail, painfully. The vast tithe barn of Hampshire or Essex, with its peg tiled roof visibly rippling along the line of split chestnut lathes beneath, its cathedral spaces arcaded in fine oak carpentry still functional enough for agricultural storage space is reduced to a back-cloth. At the rate of a hundred a year, the image clothes another out-of-town supermarket, a rigid, highly serviced shell for the display, sales and dispersal of goods.

Here is an experienced architectural practice telling the media about its proposed new discount shopping centre just off the M40. "We have created...architecture which reflects existing styles and materials... We wanted to create a development which would blend with and enhance the local environment... To this end, the buildings are rural in style... The distinctive personality of the scheme is that of an English village street with its mixture of cottage style shops and premises modelled on traditional rural industries, such as the traditional blacksmith's shop. Our remit was to reflect the brand values of a sophisticated tenant mix."

Such nonsense, reiterated dozens of times weekly in planning applications clogging up the local authority planning office in-tray, is smiled upon in the planning committee. Members have to keep the voters happy, whatever their advising officers may think, while at head office of the grocery giants, the tweedy imagery assists in the tricky balancing act of selling traditional apples, fresh baked bread and organic meat, in a space that looks like an aircraft hangar and feels like a cold store.

Similar marketing strategies apply in the volume house builders' office. New houses? Roof them in toning composite slates, give them a panel of flintwork to be seen from the road, drop in a course or two of contrasting brickwork.

Planning consent is facilitated by a nod to the "vernacular" and house prices, at least until recently, could support the extra labour involved. Adopting the superficialities of the local vernacular and adapting it to modern technology, materials and building regulations is quite feasible and sells houses.

Few question the illogicality of applying useless trim to houses built to identical standards. The functional nature of materials and techniques - tile-hanging to protect rough and ready brickwork, soft plaster to weather-proof wandering mudmade walls, slates set to bounce the rainwater off a chimney or elsewhere, feet-thick rubble walls to minimise the extremes of temperature - is long forgotten.

Forgotten too is the logic of siting. The farmhouse tucked close to the spring line, the house which sheltered in the lee of a hillside to avoid the prevailing wind, the use of existing gradients to help with drainage in farm buildings all arose from local knowledge, traditional wisdom.

Yet where that wisdom might still be of some practical use, it is overlooked. New housing is built on old water meadows - giving rise to much consternation when the flood waters rise in spring. The close knit grouping of houses for shelter and protection from the elements in coastal or exposed northern sites is abandoned. The determination to be detached, at all costs, together with official concern that car and lorry turning circles remain sacrosanct, does little for the existing, locally distinct, pattern of over-expanded towns and villages.

Superficial neo-traditionalism has gone a long way towards destroying and devaluing precisely the traditional qualities that professionals and the lay public alike believe that they are safeguarding so carefully. The paradox is that fear of homogenised architecture and building styles has led to homogenised architecture and building styles.

Design Guides, the 1970s panacea, are only as helpful as the quality of the information they convey can make them. A list of guidelines, just as provided by some 18th century landowners (for example at Whitehaven, in Cumbria), can lay down the rudiments of an urban design strategy usefully. Yet only a proper understanding of detail, form and content of a given spot will allow any useful links to be established between the locality of then and now.

The problem does not lie with those who design and commission prestige buildings. Michael Hopkins' cutlery factory for David Mellor and Evans and Shalev's Tate of the West in St Ives (both, coincidentally, standing on the site of disused gas holders) illustrate the exceptions that, sadly, cannot prove the rule. Two sites, one a valley in the Derbyshire National Park, the other a sacrosanct Cornish seaside village, have served to bring out high architectural quality. The design incentives lay, it could be said, in the constraints, but here nobody, neither strong-minded clients nor architects, was faint-hearted or derivative. The character of the place has done the trick.

The vernacular trades and skills were generally confined to the distance a man on a cart could travel to and fro in a day. Historically, local distinctiveness lay in the marks of a single mason, or carpenter, as he worked for a lifetime in one place. We have not lived that way for almost a century.

Nor is local distinctiveness just a rural question. The special qualities of, say, jerry-built Georgian Bloomsbury or Victorian Leeds, are no less worthy of attention to detail, even if the detail lies more in the way a terrace turns a corner, or a square sits relative to another.

It is, of course, hard to see the special qualities of the very familiar, which simply becomes the ordinary. Observation is dulled, perception lost, familiarity breeds contempt. Life in and around the now demolished terraces of the Byker district of Newcastle was caught by a Finnish photographer in the 1970s (though their replacement was a highly successful exercise in retaining local distinctiveness, in a different but related built form). It took the Prussian cultural attaché, Herman Muthesius, to observe the particular qualities of the English house, from mansion to LCC cottage estate, in the early 1900s. Within the houses he visited he noted the organisation of daily life, seeing it all as a thorough-going social, as well as cultural, anthropologist who saw oddities no native observer would have found worthy of comment.

Inevitably, the best book ever published on the pattern and the distinctiveness of London, was written by a Dane in the early 1930s. Steen Eiler Rasmussen observed how the neutrality of the Georgian and early Victorian square, crescent or terrace was offset by the clarity of their geometrical contribution to the plan of the town and by the visual softening of the freely planted squares and gardens between them. Like Muthesius he looked at the way people lived and used their buildings. He looked at humble terraced housing. These are, he wrote "the most simple form for a house: a large box of rooms... A Londoner is so accustomed to them that he does not see anything strange in their form; but their simple lines are not a matter of course...the facades...are mere aesthetics...in comparison with the back...a functional architecture with a chimney for each house and steep roofs...the narrow house of old Gothic London ...has survived in the dwellings of the nineteenth century.."

He could apply the same clarity to a late Victorian terraced house with back extension - a house-type utterly commonplace in this country, but quite distinctive, seen from elsewhere. (If anyone doubts it, listen to the comments of observant visitors new to England, on the train from Gatwick to Victoria, as they notice, and wonder at, the arcane world of the back gardens of Purley and Tooting).

Local distinctiveness, of a particularly visual order, can be found in the once-derided holiday homes so lovingly constructed around ancient railway carriages along the Sussex coast or in the isolated pockets of thirties housing (paradoxically, the feared International Style, that would sweep all before it) that survive in the suburbs.

But, more usually, panic of the unknown, fear of the unexpected, cause us to retreat behind unsatisfactory copies of what seems familiar or typical. If a weak simalcrum of a traditional house can pass muster, similar logic accepts that a single historic facade propped against an entirely modern office block is a properly conserved building. That it does not exist, beyond that single dimension, a wall of brick or stone, is of little concern.

Yet, look along the main street of, say, Chipping Campden or Kings Lynn - rich medieval towns at either side of the country. Behind the pukka 17th and 18th century facades of stone or brick lurk the original forms and timber framed skeletons of medieval houses, stretching far back on their plots. Or look at that pleasing Georgian farmhouse, apparently so symmetrical but often just a room thick, grafted onto the pleasant jumble of an old Tudor cottage. The public face of a house was designed to show that the owner was in the van of fashion and could afford to be so - never mind what lay behind. Such confidence is the exact reverse of our nervous, fundamentally dishonest approach.

Before the 1947 Town and Country Planning Act, fear of the unknown centred upon creeping suburbanisation. The planner Thomas Sharp envisaged, on paper at least, the possibility of London smothering the Home Counties at 12 houses to the acre "and it is only a matter of time before..it will be linked up to Newcastle and Plymouth, with a beauty-spot preserved here and there, and here and there a hundred or two acres reserved as an agricultural area".

George Orwell conjured up another hellish scene; "pink villas fifty yards apart; all over those hills, as far as you can see, villa after villa, with all the gramophones playing the same tune. And all the forests shaved flat - chewed into wood-pulp for the "News of the World", or sawn up into gramophone cases."[1] In fact it was Burma but the roots of the panic were the same.

The unfettered expansion of the thirties provoked fears of a countryside smothered by development, obliterating what was special and putting nothing of note in its place. With hindsight, those reactions seem a touch hysterical. Yet despite a sophisticated panoply of safeguards, statutory control and development strategies few changes are seen as for the best.

What we have lost is a sense of judgement, based upon accurate evidence. Incremental change of detail leads to change of identity, so survival of a sense of locality must involve acceptance of renewal as well as care for what remains. The inability to absorb change is a sclerotic cultural condition.

All along the east coast in the 17th century the details and materials of Dutch traditional architecture were effortlessly digested. Dutch gables and pantiles are still there to remind us of the process. Everywhere that colonial settlers went, from the Portugese in India to the Scots in the Antipodes, people took the built forms of home and then allowed them to mingle with what they found.

Local distinctiveness lies in the detail. The proportion and fine detail of regional domestic architecture, doors, windows, pointing, even paint colour and texture. Use the wrong material or pitch for a roof, hard render instead of lime plaster, wood-stain instead of paint, let alone replacement window frames or inappropriate doors, and the quality has gone. William Morris, in the Manifesto he wrote in 1877 when founding the Society for the Protection of Ancient Buildings compared the restoration of a damaged painting, "where the partly-perished work of the ancient craftsmaster has been made neat and smooth by the tricky hand of some unoriginal and thoughtless hack of today," with the restoration, as opposed to the repair, of old buildings.

Sometimes a clear idea of period is the essential notion; at other times, the key is timelessness - perhaps the hardest quality of all to achieve, for every period film shows its date. The basic house type of the eastern seaboard of the USA, painted weatherboard (clapboard) and pitched shingled roof is scarcely marked by the era in which it was built.Its origins lie somewhere in Northern Europe, but such roots have been lost in the American soil. It can be dismantled, added to, treated almost as a kit of parts, for the pattern is familiar to everyone who works on such buildings and there are few unknown factors. Such accommodating design becomes an adjustable model, easily adaptable to modern demand for insulation, special glazing or other needs.

Other patternbook approaches, such as the way in which each Victorian railway company chose an architectural style and then used it as a house style up and down its tracks, have produced different versions of local distinctiveness. The Jacobean style of the Staffordshire line or the picturesque Gothic Revival of the Settle to Carlisle stations were marketing strategies, ploys to make the identity of that line distinct. A lesson for the supermarket chains here, perhaps?

In much the same way, the major estate owners built their cottages, model farms and, even villages, in a "house style", sometimes simply consisting of a recognisable pattern of glazing bars or just a noticeable paint colour. A monogram and datestone set into the gable end or over the porch, told the visitor who owned what locally.

Local distinctiveness in architectural terms as otherwise is not about freezing the frame, nor about slavish imitation of a kit of parts. It is about perception, of the detail, pattern and texture of place - the spaces in between the buildings as much as the buildings. The loss of that distinctiveness can lie in some blind logic, such as the remorseless filling of the "village envelope", leaving no breathing space, no views outwards. It can be lost by blotting out the urban rhythm, denting the pattern, pulling a coherent street apart with an American-style shopping mall or vast garage forecourt.

For those who have in recent years tried designing new settlements, in whatever style and wherever in the country, a plethora of regulations, relating to roads, access, servicing and the rest, make the job almost impossible. For example, it is impossible to design a formal road pattern (often the bones of 18th and 19th century planned villages) since traffic must always filter and roads never cross.

In the late '80s a few honest attempts were made to design small new settlements with a sense of place - whilst hundreds more "new villages" missed the point altogether. Not one has succeeded, though that most laboured and persistent of all efforts, the Prince of Wales' Poundbury, on Duchy of Cornwall land outside Dorchester, has finally achieved planning permission for a first small segment. Leon Krier as masterplanner drew up an elaborate Building Code, "to inspire, inform and encourage as much as regulate and prohibit. It was intended to creat a cultural climate in which builders could devise acceptable solutions of their own in the hope that some of the inventive vigour of authentic vernacular might emerge."[2] Despite the careful framing of the Code, its length and precision, now that the first phase is due to go on site, the Code has been overtaken by a two-tier arrangement of architects, working closely with the builders. When the most conscientious effort yet seen to produce a vernacular revival came to the test, the skills and traditional understanding was found wanting. To go back to the beginning is no answer.

Out in the real world, developers cling to their market-led image of a house that sells. A visit to the Ideal Home Exhibition amply reinforces the notion that volume house builders, and those that follow where they lead, have nailed their feet to the ground and shut their eyes. They have found a tradition, ersatz as it is, and are sticking to it.

In the 1970s, when I first began to write about housing, local authorities around the country were commissioning small housing schemes in town or village which often incorporated essential regional patterns - whether of grouping, finish and materials, or detail. They were, at best, welcome additions to the scene - often also involving the rehabilitation of run-down older buildings. Most of that experience has been dissipated as offices were disbanded, practices turned to commercial schemes. In recent years there have been a few imaginative housing association schemes (usually urban) which follow the same broad principles but the political and economic climate does not favour them and the future looks even less promising.

Local distinctiveness is elusive, easy to lose and difficult to find. Not fixed in some golden age, it is, on the contrary, here and now. It was always so.

William Morris puts it best; "every change, whatever history it destroyed, left history in the gap, and was alive with the spirit of the deeds done midst its fashioning." That, eloquently put, is the germ of local distinctiveness, the traditional and the contemporary working together to endorse a sense of place.

References
1 Dennis Hardy and Colin Ward, *Arcadia for All*, London, 1984
2 Dan Cruickshank, The Independent, 26 May 1993.

Local Distinctiveness:
on the Curiosities and Perils of the
English Approach
Patrick Wright

Divided as the British may be on many issues, we are surely almost all in favour of local distinctiveness. The idea seems to command immediate loyalty up and down the land, and it has the peculiar attraction - especially compelling at a time when so many are convinced of the futility and decadence of conventional politics - of doing so without demanding that people settle their differences. Under this flag the Yorkshire miner can apparently come to terms with the Surrey stockbroker, the urban slum dweller with the rural squire. In the name of local distinctiveness, we may even imagine the English stepping out from under the cover of the unitary British state to hold their own smaller patch of ground alongside the already well differentiated Welsh and Scots.

But if it is one thing to raise the standard for this most timely of causes, it is another to be sure exactly what 'local distinctiveness' amounts to as a cause at the end of the twentieth century. We might say that it is about the unique quality of places and their particular cultures. We might describe it as the opposite of a shopping mall, a MacDonalds and perhaps even a National Trust shop too. But a teasing vagueness still clings to the term: indeed, as we attempt to define it more closely, we find ourselves wandering through an exotic anthology of almost lost causes. If local distinctiveness is about the varied flora and fauna of the landscape, it also seems to emanate from lamp-posts, trolley buses and allotments. While it is much concerned with architecture, it also has to do with particular cheeses, gas-holders, barred gates, kippers and increasingly scarce dialect words. It may be about local stone, pargeting and thatch, but then, as I discovered on a recent drive through East Anglia, it is also a matter of corrugated iron, baling twine, and perhaps even US Airforce bases too. On east London's Dalston Lane, meanwhile, it may not accept the drab-looking public library, named after the C.L.R. James, the late West Indian historian, revolutionary and cricket writer, but it surely embraces the misapprehension which has some locals assuming that those letters C.L.R. stand for Councillor James.

To make matters more perplexing, local distinctiveness has a philosophical dimension too. Indeed, it is much concerned with the meaning of meaning, with the relation between apparently distinct things, and with the equally complicated matter of being at home in the world. Local distinctiveness is inclined to take the side of 'authenticity' against artifice, administration and the all pervading televisual image. It seems to prefer intuition to literal-minded fact. It favours things that have been in the same place for a very long time, and all the more so if no public authority or entrepreneur has yet got round to sticking up a notice drawing attention to this fact. Its advocates are strongly in agreement with the French critic who said of EuroDisney that the difference between a proper city and a theme park is that a city has ghosts. There can be no doubt where local distinctiveness stands in that contest: it takes the side of ghosts against anybody's themed experience or crafty manipulation of appearances, and it feels decidedly ambivalent about the kind of self-consciousness that tourism and other 'leisure-related development strategies' bring to the identity of places.

We can sharpen our understanding of this diffuse term, and identify something of the challenge facing those who would make a cause of it now, by considering its emergence at earlier times in the English twentieth century. I confine my comments to the English experience not because I consider it generally representative, but because that is the particular inheritance with which we have to deal.

Others have certainly been here before. To begin with, we might remember Ian Nairn, a fighting architectural conservationist of the fifties and sixties. In 1955 he organised a special issue of the Architectural Review, a magazine with which John Betjeman was also associated. The issue, which was called Outrage, contained a comprehensive attack on the diverse forces that were burying the English landscape in a mediocre uniformity. 'Subtopia', so Nairn wrote in that issue, is 'the annihilation of the site, the steamrollering of all individuality of place to one uniform and mediocre pattern'. Nairn worried that 'if what is called development is allowed to multiply at the present rate, then by the end of the century Great Britain will consist of isolated oases of preserved monuments in a desert of wire, concrete roads, cosy plots and bungalows'. He feared that there would be 'no real distinction between town and country', for both would consist of a limbo of shacks, bogus rusticities, wire and aerodromes, set in some fir-poled field'. Drawn up only a few years after the Second World War, his list of Subtopia's agents has a certain period charm. It includes arterial roads, ribbon development, wire, dumping grounds, and military installations.

He was in no doubt that 'any type of military installation' could have been chosen to illustrate the threat, since 'they all reproduce the same pattern' of 'new extensions and old derelictions', but airfields were worst of all because only they 'impinge on the countryside as well as the land'.

Ten or fifteen years previously, a spirited defence of local quality was mounted by those pioneers of organic farming who eventually came together as founding members of the Soil Association in 1946. These people were far-sighted in many ways. They worried about soil erosion and the woeful inadequacy of the industrialised urban diet, and they wanted to see many more people living on the land. They argued, with an early 'preventative' emphasis, that the orientation of the new National Health Service should be shifted from sickness to health, and that agriculture should be counted as 'one of the health services'.[1] They were critical of the way mechanisation was being used to concentrate profits and reduce agricultural employment; and also of the new agricultural marketing boards with which the state seemed only to be increasing the distance between local producers and consumers, while lining the pockets of powerful distributors. As one veteran remembers, the heart of the organic movement of that time was committed to a 'defence of locality' - based on the 'hypothesis that health would be built up on the local.' [2] They wanted fewer imports and a greater commitment to home agriculture, an increase in livestock, the decentralisation of industry and the re-opening of local mills and slaughter houses.

As with Ian Nairn's attack on Subtopia, the Soil Association's attempt to resurrect the local was mounted in the face of opposition that seemed hugely powerful and overwhelming. One can sense this in Lady Eve Balfour's insistence that the health of the nation was more important than the profits and share dividends of any large combine, that the 'new world order' of the post-war planners must be extended to take proper account of the soil, and that the prevailing idea of 'the conquest of nature' was of the same order as 'the Nazi conquest of Europe'. The pesticide and herbicide revolution had yet to take off, but even before that was added to her troubles, Lady Balfour was in no doubt that the soil would die unless 'the false idols of comfort and money' were dethroned. She concluded, with a characteristic mixture of desperation and determined upper class pluck, that the restoration of locality could only really come with the restoration of Christian society, and that this meant avoiding the Nazi ideology of 'deifying the state'.

We can follow the emerging cause of local distinctiveness further back into the thirties. This was a decade in which doughty English villagers opposed the Post Office's imposition of red telephone boxes into their communities, condemning these amenities - which are now defended as vital features of the landscape and, indeed, the very emblems of local distinctiveness - as a monstrously uniform 'intervention of red' into the locally diverse national scene. It also produced the artists who were commissioned in the early years of the war to paint pictures for the Recording Britain Scheme. Employed to portray the cherished Britain that was threatened by the Nazis, they travelled through the counties and, following the advice of the CPRE, came up with a singular contribution to the war effort - a collection of images of a country that had apparently already gone to war with all that was best in itself: villages threatened by ribbon development, valleys threatened by municipal reservoirs, houses threatened by insensitive local authority regulations about what was fit for human habitation, a few mansions sunk into military and 'institutional' use.

That was also a time when the diverse charms of the traditional British landscape and forest were being vigorously defended against the improving endeavours of the state. The Forestry Commission, which had been set up shortly after the First World War and charged with ensuring that Britain never again suffered the kind of timber shortage that had come with the German submarine blockade, was under especially vehement criticism. The idea had been to plant a 'strategic reserve' of timber which would, so the original commission hoped, enable the country to be self-sufficient in timber for three years. Within a few years the Commission was under attack for imposing coniferous monoculture that really did seem to threaten what Ian Nairn would later call 'the annihilation of the site'.

Much of this criticism was fully justified, as will be obvious to anyone who has visited the Commission's Sitka plantations in the Scottish uplands, or counted up the acres of ancient woodland that were poisoned and converted into conifer plantations, or looked at Forestry Commission journals from that period and noticed their enthusiastic advocacy of ploughing up what are now protected as rare heaths. However, it also flared into bizarre demonisation. The Commission's conifers became an army of invasion, marching in rows over the native British landscape. The symbolism used by the critics of the pre-war Forestry Commission could be wild, excessive and detached from reality. The fact that the Commission adopted methods of plantation forestry from the German tradition of silviculture, gave its critics licence to revile this new statutory body as a kind of silvicultural Fifth Column and planter of Huns. The historian G.M. Trevelyan led the National Trust into a battle for the Lake District, claiming, reasonably enough, that the introduction of the conifer was 'a crime against Nature's local bye-laws', but then protesting altogether more emotively, that the English fell should not be converted into 'German pine Forest'.[3] H.J. Massingham, a major defender of the countryside in that interwar period, also took a somewhat frantic line on this subject, condemning the Commission for taking a place like the Breckland in south-west Norfolk (ironically, now one of the Forestry Commission's conservation showcases) and turning it into 'a parade ground for conifers, equidistant, each the spit of its brother and all of them set out in standardized rows as though the voice of Nature had just bawled "Attention! "'[4]

We may well now smile at the excesses of this language, deriving as it does from a time before conservation had gained institutional power, and when it could only proceed by turning up the rhetoric and projecting its horror at this particular form of state intervention right back into Nature itself. But if that was the thirties, our own custodians of the indigenous landscape are not entirely free of polemical habit. I recently heard of a National Trust forester who had looked at a shelter belt in north Dorset and regretting that the whitebeam in it would have to go - unfortunately it was Swedish whitebeam, and therefore unworthy of its place on the English downs. As for the poor sycamore, this may be Prince Charles's favourite tree, but there are conservationists who revile it too as an alien imposter - an illegal immigrant with leaves on. Objectors are still hurling the Germanic accusation at the Forestry Commission's conifers too, an activity that must surely be considered reckless now that a financially embarrassed government is eyeing up the Forestry Commission, which has learned much from its critics in recent years, as a candidate for privatisation.

*****

I do not raise these old arguments in order to discredit the idea of local distinctiveness as it concerns us now, but rather because I think we should take the measure of these earlier manifestations in order to avoid falling into old pitfalls. For the better part of the century, local distinctiveness has been seen as a fundamentally defensive cause. Indeed, it has had the desperate quality of a beleaguered resistance movement, and its heroism has belonged to the last ditch. That temptation is available in our time too, since the threats to local distinctiveness continue to add up to a formidable gallimaufry of centralising, place-annulling forces. We can all draw up our own lists, taking our pick from such things as the centralised media, the many agencies and programmes of the modern state, both national and European, the Common Agricultural Policy, herbicides and pesticides, health and safety regulations, the school system, with its elevation of Standard English over local dialect, the motor car with its endless roads, the supermarkets and chainstores, which own some 60% of retail outlets in Britain as compared with 26% in Italy, a country which is famous for the diversity of its towns.[5]

But if the place-annulling forces of uniformity are as rampant as ever, we should avoid the temptation of the hopeless headlong charge. For it is that sort of thing that has previously led the cause of local distinctiveness to develop morbidities of its own. Its beleaguered advocates have shown a pronounced tendency towards archaism, extending their forlorn hopes only to such relics and residues as have somehow survived the coming of modern administration, and seeing nothing in the new except degeneration and further destruction. They have identified their cause with the defence of a traditional way of rural life that few if any people are really prepared to live any more, and they have been inclined towards a dangerously simplified view of the forces constellating the society in which they have lived.

The fact is that if you reject the state, commerce, industrialisation, and every other modern energy in sight you are left to build your house with very strange materials indeed. Even those who see more in New Agery than a few quirky ideas, will surely wonder about the associations that clustered around the cause of local distinctiveness in the thirties. Some of the most committed pre-war advocates - people who were really prescient on some ecological issues - combined their defence of English local life with fascist sympathies; others were influenced by theories of a Jewish financial conspiracy; and many, who didn't sign up for these morbid simplifications, were still content to use a dismissive symbolism of bureaucrats, commissars, plutocratic chain-store owners, and Hunlike conifers all in a row.

We should probably not make too much of these mid-century failings, but anyone who thinks it is gratuitous or obscure of me to raise these spectres from the thirties, should drop in on W.H. Smiths and pick up a copy of *This England*. Here is a heritage quarterly with reputed sales of 160,000 per issue, which is precisely concerned with the local distinctiveness of the English scene: the historical quality of towns and counties; the traditional arts and crafts of the countryside; and an endless fantasia about thatching, steam engines and the charisma of undiminished Royalty which has been running since the late sixties.

Much of this magazine is inoffensive, although its image of the countryside leans heavily on dead cliché. Yet it has a decidedly unpleasant undercurrent which flows in directly from the murkiest depths of the prewar imagination I have been talking about. This sometimes spills out in the editorials, but it is displayed in less restrained form on the letters page where ex-pats and other affronted patriots leave no doubt at all that the distinctiveness of *This England* is that it offers no quarter to coloured immigrants, long-haired students, trade union barons and homosexuals. In recent issues, the 'Forever England' column has been written by one Stuart Millson, a former member of the British National Party who leaves no doubt as to what he means when he raises the fallen flag of St. George.

To take up the cause of local distinctiveness now must also be to redefine it so that it is not available to this sort of abuse. We must break with the lugubrious archaism that would confine local distinctiveness to the vaults of ancestral fantasy. This will certainly mean making the most of the fact that the state is now available as an instrument of conservation rather than just its enemy, but it also demands that we conceive local distinctiveness in open, dynamic and contemporary terms - and certainly not as something that must be protected from every manifestation of modernity.

Some of those old veterans I have been discussing knew this very well. Ian Nairn was right when he said 'To re-use a palace as the town's post office is better than turning it into a museum'.[6] The same point was made by Wilfrid Hiley, a forest economist who was among those who defended the Forestry Commission in the early thirties. As he wrote 'The danger of "preservation" is that in killing the disease it will also kill the patient and that the relics of the countryside, duly and reverentially embalmed, will be preserved as a mummy for the admiration of future tourists'.[7] As he adds, 'In contrast to the mummification of the country is the intensification if its vitality, which comes from the vigorous pursuit of rural industries.' To this we can only agree. Mummification is definitely not the answer. If it is to mean anything useful, local distinctiveness must be about activity and interaction, not just design or antiquarian romance. It must be about places that have something going for them - not just identical neo-Victorian bollards in every street.

We are familiar with the excesses that can be committed in the name of heritage, but those who were concerned to defend the traditions of country life in Britain during the twenties and thirties, also had to fight against certain artificial conceptions of their cause. Some of them lived in a state of open war with the weekend cottage, and were defiantly proud of their own unpicturesque and certainly not thatched dwellings. They asserted the true facts of rural poverty against the false charms of the picturesque, which H.J. Massingham described as a slug that had smeared the countryside over - emptying it of people and vitality, from the enclosures onwards, and leaving nothing but a few brow-beaten and torpid agricultural workers and a touristic view. In the phrase of J. W. Robertson Scott, the founder of *The Countryman*, the challenge was to cut through the 'pleasant seeming' in order to emphasise the 'haggard reality beneath'.

In this respect their defence of the locale holds many messages for us. Too much of what is done in the name of heritage has the same place-annulling effect as the picturesque. In its excesses, indeed, the system of environmental exploitation that sometimes goes by the name of Heritage has become another agent of Subtopia. Whether we be talking about neo-Victorian street furniture, which is identical from one historical centre to another, or the systems of interpretation that make one heritage display so much like another, it has become abundantly clear in recent years that, badly handled, the very sign of local distinctiveness can become an enemy of the very quality to which it draws attention. Nairn may have disapproved of the functional concrete lamp standards of the fifties, but it is hard to imagine him feeling hugely relieved by the equally identical fake Victorian ones with which so many of them are now being replaced.

Conservation will properly remain a permanent concern, but we must see to it that local distinctiveness is also a contemporary quality, connected to the life, skills and intelligence of the present, and certainly not just a marketing strategy. Without that we will have little more than relics on the one hand, and self conscious whimsy - of the sort associated with bad public art - on the other: quirky indulgences which, in the absence of any serious cultural ground, will seem arbitrary and self-indulgent.

Common Ground has already carried out some adjustments in the repertoire: or so we may gather from the inclusion of mosques and gasholders in its recently published local distinctiveness poster. But we must be prepared to make further changes to the traditional distribution of the virtue we are calling local distinctiveness. All places have their qualities, as we know, but some more than others.... There is, to this day, power in that preference. If MacDonalds opens in Bath or Stratford, they will adjust their signage - this may be a condition of getting in - but they won't do any such thing in Dalston or Luton. Previous admirers of local quality have favoured old villages, historic towns and the countryside. The reforming state and commerce were reviled, but large tracts of the modern nation were simply consigned to the oubliette: most of the city, the places of industry, the new towns, the suburbs - these were simply left off the map of local distinctiveness, and they must be reinstated.

I will end with a point made by Stephen Jay Gould, the evolutionary biologist who is nothing if not awed by the extent of natural diversity. Reflecting on his own preference for authenticity - which he associates with cable cars, old pancake parlours, etc. - he also points out the impracticality of 'a strict aesthetic of maximal diversity'. This, as he says, would produce chaos - and it was quite reasonable that the 'criteria of design', whether they be concerned with roads, telephone systems or anything else, should have a universality about them. This point reminds us that it would be romantic nonsense to value local distinctiveness without addressing the question of commonality as well. Gould reckons that what matters about the universal framework is that it should be

sufficiently open to accomodate distinctive local traditions. He illustrates his
point by comparing McDonalds with the older American institution of the
Diner - a rail-car turned into a restaurant and McDonalds.[8] The Diner was
manufactured in 'a few standardized sizes and shapes', but the owners then
went on to customise and distinguish them, bringing in local products,
individual staff, and building a clientele which could well become 'a community of common care'. McDonalds, meanwhile, worked in the opposite way -
entering 'the small-scale domain of appropriate uniqueness', and unfolding its
own show of 'crushing uniformity' in which nothing resembling a distinct
community was likely to develop.

For Gould nature finds its correlative more in the hubbub and mix of the city
than in the countryside, where generations of contemplative pastoralists have
preferred to place it. The latter may treat the city as the great wen, but Gould
is full of enthusiasm for those densely populated parts of the city where worlds
intersect on the street corner, where nothing can with absolute certainty be
fixed to a single meaning, and where discontinuity rather than ancient
settlement is the norm. That is what local distinctiveness is really all about -
even if no-one has yet figured out how to stick a sign on it.

References
1.   Quoted from Lady Eve Balfour, *TheLivingSoil*, London, 1944.
2.   I quote from Mary Langman, who was secretary to the doctors at the
     organic Pioneer Healthy Centre in Peckham before the war, and has
     been involved with the Soil Association since the early days.
3.   Quoted from David Cannadine, *G.M Trevelyan; a life in history*,
     HarperCollins, 1992, p. 156.
4.   See the article entitled 'England Laid Waste', in H.J. Massingham's
     The Heritage of Man, Jonathan Cape, 1929, p.301.
5.   I owe this information to the Comedia Consultancy Group.
6.   Ian Nairn, *'Counter-Attack'*, Architectural Review, December 1956.
7.   W.E. Hiley, *Improvement of Woodlands*, Country Life, 1931.
8.   See 'Counters and Cable Cars' in Stephen Jay Gould, *Eight Little
     Piggies; Reflections in Natural History,* Jonathan Cape, 1993,
     pp. 238-248.
     Emanuel Litvinoff, *Journey through a Small Planet*, Robin Clarke,
     1972/93

The Failure of the Melting Pot
Neal Ascherson

When I reflect on local distinctiveness - the reality which lies in memory, rather than the concept - I find that I think first about bread.

The best white bread I ever ate was served with a foul lunch in a hotel at Feodosia, a port on the Crimean coast. When I remember those broad, crusty, slightly yellowish slices I also remember that the very best bread wheat of the ancient world was grown in that Black Sea steppe to feed Athens and Rome, and later Constantinople and Venice, and eventually (until the coming of cheap prairie wheat from north America) Victorian Britain. The best black bread to come my way is (was?) the huge black rye loaves which are sold in the early morning, still almost too hot to touch, out of the back of the bakery on Basanavicius Street in Vilnius, the capital of Lithuania. These loaves, still edible a fortnight later, perfumed my hotel room with a scent of caraway and ferment and warm sleeping babies. I took one to Warsaw and gave it to a Polish novelist born in Vilnius, to bring back to him, through taste and smell, the colours and sounds of his Lithuanian boyhood.

In this sense, a good pilgrimage shrine for local distinctiveness is the Bread Museum at Ulm, in Swabia. Here, dignified but fossilised on the shelves, are loaves to show that every town and village and monastery in southern Germany once baked in its own style and shape and mixture. But even in the vocabulary which I have used so far ("pathetic", "memory", "once"), there has crept in the assumption which underlies all discussion of local distinctiveness: that it is passing away. "They used to bake for themselves; on the fringes of the European continent or in its less developed hills or remote islands, they still do; but soon they will do so no longer...."

It is not so simple. We are in the grip of processes which are not complementary but contradictory. When I was a child, a fair number of the men and women and their children who lived in the Highlands and Islands of Scotland wore clothes made up from cloth or wool which they had woven or knitted themselves. Many of them spoke Gaelic in the kitchen, though not usually before strangers. But, at the same time, they ate repulsive Glasgow bread, gas-bleached and many days old, brought in by boat, and when they could afford it they consumed tinned Canadian salmon, pilchard or snoek rather than the fresh mackerel, saithe and whiting which abounded in the sea beside them. They listened respectfully to radio programmes made exclusively in English and almost entirely for the English.

The picture today has changed. But it has not changed in a simple linear development from what existed then. Almost everybody wears standard urban clothing: jeans, trainers, anoraks, imported jerseys. Almost nobody speaks Gaelic any more, except in the Western Isles. But, on the other hand, Gaelic is now abundantly available throughout the Highlands and Islands in dedicated television and radio programming, in the schoolroom, in bookshops, in sections of local newspapers and - in some places - in bilingual signposting. A number of small local bakeries have appeared, distributing excellent and varied breads by bus or van. Oatmeal, for centuries the staple of the Gaeltacht after it replaced rye or bere, became almost totally unobtainable during the 1970s as crofters stopped growing it, but it has now reappeared in many small Highland towns. It is to be found in Health Food shops, displayed in sacks alongside mung beans and low-calorie muesli. As for the inshore sea, it is now so ruthlessly over-fished and its floor so brutally scraped by clam-dredgers that it is in danger of becoming lifeless.

Local distinctiveness, then, appears to be at once declining and recovering. Part of the explanation lies in demographic changes. Those who open small bakeries or organic groceries or shops for the fibre-minded tend to be "white settler" incomers; usually young, usually English, refugees from outer London or the post-industrial cities of northern England. With those who are responsible for the revival of Gaelic as a medium of education and communication, it is more complicated. Some, but relatively few, of the initiators come from a Gaelic-speaking family background on the West Coast or in the Isles. Substantially more are Scots who have with varying success set themselves to learn the language as adults, from backgrounds which may be urban-Lowland or non-Gaelic Highland.

The Gaelic-speaking population on the ground clearly appreciate this revival. But they seem to perceive it as a gift bestowed from outside rather than as a response to any expressed demands or needs of their own.

The motives of the language-revivers are in part political. Most of them share a conviction that the Gaelic language revival contributes to the cultural self-confidence of a Scotland seeking to rebuild its identity. There is also a "moral" element: anxiety that a culture is rapidly approaching extinction before its "ancient" and "unique" values can be saved for posterity. Lastly, no doubt, there is a degree of honest ambition. Murderous attacks have been recently hurled at this so-called "Gaelic Mafia" on the grounds that it is a self-promoting, overpaid intellectual clique with no real connection to the surviving Gaelic community. I cannot agree with that at all, but it would be wrong to get into that particular row. The point of mentioning it is only to demonstrate the ironies at work in these cross-currents of change.

These specific ironies, about what happens in one part of Scotland, are evidence towards a general theory: that the melting-pot is broken. The impression of a world in which differences between groups are diminishing in a simple way is delusive. Instead, the world - human culture - is simultaneously both uniting and comminuting. It is becoming more uniform and less uniform, at once coagulating into larger entities and breaking down into smaller ones.

The melting-pot image was invented to describe the process by which the United States successively assimlated wave after wave of immigrants - English, Scots-Irish, German, Jewish, Italian, Slav - into a single American identity. This image was always inadequate. It ignored the non-assimilation of two groups, the indigenous "Indians" and the descendants of imported black slaves. But after the end of the Second World War, under the shelter of the Pax Americana, the melting-pot image began to be marketed across the "democratic world" as a model of how nation-states containing several cultures should develop.

This ideal was not just an extrapolation from American experience. It was one more version of 20th century "statism": the assumption that to be successful a state must rule over a population which was as far as possible homogenous. In pre-1945 Europe, this assumption had lead to the use of terror and genocide against "alien" and minority cultures. Immediately after 1945, it helped to justify the expulsion of something like twelve million Germans, above all from the newly-acquired territories of Poland and from Czechoslovakia. In post-war western Europe, in a new climate of "Christian Democracy", the urge to homogeneity expressed itself in a much more benign way: the principle, written into the German Basic Law for example, that a state's duty was to equalise living standards throughout its territory. But all these manifestations related to the same premise: that an advanced society was one in which differences of all kinds - local, religious, racial, linguistic, differences of class - were being melted down into a "higher" unity.

It is that premise which has ceased to be convincing. The traditional nation-state is breaking down, and so, very plainly, is the melting-pot which it invented. Few want to mend it.

But before discussing these breakdowns, which became so spectacular after 1989, it is important to go back for a moment to the elements: bread, clothes, language. Any partisan of local distinctiveness has to defend herself or himself against the charge of reactionary sentimentalism. These day, this charge is brought by a particular kind of analysis of centre-periphery relations, which runs like this:

1.   Cultural change starts from the centre and spreads ouwards. The process resembles rings spreading from a stone thrown into water. They travel across the middle of the pond to the bank/periphery, where they finally vanish.

2.   Thus it is possible to see at the periphery things (customs or values, artefacts, varieties of bread) still in use which have long passed out of use at the centre. Because they are at the periphery, they are about to cease their outward journey and disappear for ever.

3.   Romantics at the centre, unaware of the "spreading rings" process, think that the periphery was always, immemorially, as it now appears. They assume, for example, that bagpipes and Sabbatarianism are intrinsically "Highland". They miss the fact that both once formed part of the culture of "core" northern Europe and thence spread in local variants to reach the periphery, where they survived centuries after the Germans, the English or the Dutch began to go over to the piano and the concertina, and half a century after most Protestant countries surrendered to the "Continental Sunday".

The same is true of the Celtic languages, which probably arrived in west-central Europe in the second millenium BC. They survive in Brittany, Wales and parts of Ireland and Scotland not because those regions are essentially "Celtic" but because they are essentially peripheral. The next linguistic ripples, French and English, have reached that Atlantic fringe of Europe and are now threatening to push the Celtic languages into extinction.

4.   For the central intellectual, the local distinctiveness of the periphery becomes important for two reasons: because it is distinct - it is unlike the central culture - and because, with nowhere further to go, it is about to vanish. The culture of the fringe is seen, falsely, as "original" and therefore more natural and healthy. The bread is more fibrous, the languages are more expressive and beautiful, relationships are more sincere, individuality is more respected than in the grim, uniform streets of the centre. And all this is under threat. The cry goes up: Save it! Stop history! Make it un-happen!

I have spelt out this argument at length, because it matters. It is saying that interest in local distinctiveness is always preservative - always to some degree an attempt to slow or stop the unstoppable historical process. This kind of centre-periphery analysis certainly has a lot of debunking merits. But as a system, it contains its own bugs. First, it is Britocentric. The model of concentric waves does not easily fit the European mainland, "their backwardness" could be geographically central and where there has been a profusion of major and minor centres. Second, it ignores the dialectic nature of the process, in which the past (recovered, saved or reinvented) reacts against the present to form the future. Take this bread question again. Once there was a time when most reasonably-off households in say Inveraray made their own bread. Then came the invention of the plant bakery which could mass-produce a standard loaf and distribute it from Glasgow over a huge area. Finally, urban refugees settling in small towns like Inveraray begin to produce a simulation of home-baked bread in small batches for local consumption - but using technologies actually more sophisticated than the methods of the 1950s plant bakery.

The attempt to renew the past engenders the new and different future. In the same way, the breakdown of large societal units into smaller ones - into localities - only superficially resembles older patterns of community, and in fact introduces quite new ones.

This is what took place when the melting-pot broke. A few people, by 1989, did expect the fall of the external Soviet empire and even predicted the approaching end of the Soviet Union. But even they assumed that the general trend toward uniformity and bigness would continue. It is worth recalling four massive illusions which dominated our thinking, in the saloon-bar or the academic common-room, up to 1989.

1.   "The world is solidifying into two or possibly three superpowers, with the rest of humanity as their back gardens." This illusion arose from Cold War conditions. The existence of nuclear weapons appeared to be a supreme fact which would impose growing political conformity and subordination upon the planet.

2.   "The world is a global village, in which uniformity of communication, popular culture and consumption will inevitably lead to uniformity of political structures." This proposition is the descendant of a much older one about language, which assumed that "when everyone speaks English (or French or Esperanto) there will be no more point in nationalism".

The utter wrongness of all this is now blatant. Those who led the revolutions in eastern Europe or Russia wore fake Fruit of the Loom T-shirts, threw Coca-Cola cans and kept an eye on CNN. Boris Yeltsin, besieged in Moscow during the 1991 putsch, was nourished by a nearby Pizza Hut. In other words, uniformity of desire does not slake the lust for political diversity but appears to inflame it. The leader of nationalist movements turned out to be precisely those whose taste in clothes, pop music and diet was most "global". As for language, it should have been obvious from 1848 on, if not from 1789, that people who become able to communicate in a *Weltsprache* like English or French grow thereby more revolutionary, and more determined to throw off the foreign yoke, rather than less.

3.   "The growth of multinational corporations, deciding everything that matters from remote boardrooms in Los Angeles or Frankfurt, drains all meaning from the existence of nations - especially new, small ones." Few people remember this line of argument now, immensely popular in the 1970s. The multinationals have entirely failed to steer world politics, if they ever wished to do so. Their influence may be noxious, but it remains mostly limited to the market place and politicians have lost much of their fear of it. On the contrary, the imagined political menace of the multinationals has stimulated rather than asphyxiated nationlist and regionalist politics.

4.   "Liberal capitalism, now apparently the unchallenged future of the human race, is a unifying and standardising force. Its monopoly, when complete, will render adversarial politics irrelevant." But capitalism is both unifier and divider at once . It presses towards a single world market, and towards the consolidation of production into fewer and bigger units. But it also sets up violent stresses which can shatter larger political systems into smaller ones: the dynamics of uneven development and envious local aspiration. Anyway, capitalism for the moment exists in several different sub-species. Its structure and ethic are different in Britain, Germany, Japan and so on. There is a sense in which the nation is still dictating the form of capitalism - and not the other way round.

After 1989, the falsity of these "one-world" predictions became apparent, above all in Europe. In the East, the Soviet empire was replaced by a multiplicity of nation-states, some with claims to revive a previous independence and others - like Ukraine and Belarus - quite new. In a second phase, some of these nation-states then began to subdivide: peacefully in Czechoslovakia; violently in Bosnia. In the West, the end of the Cold War accelerated the decline of nation-states, which leaked authority upwards to "federal" institutions at Brussels or Strasbourg but also downwards to the powerul regionalist movement.

At the same time, the concept of "metropolis" or "centre" went into decline. The regional upsurge is challenging the traditional status of the "capital city". As the Scottish thinker Tom Nairn has written, "there are no more imperial capitals in the old high ideological sense - no Vienna, no Paris, no modern Byzantium or world-city to impose its suzerainty of culture, tongue and fashion. Post-1989, there is unlikely to be such a centre again". He might have added London to the list. The city continues to drain wealth and power out of the rest of Britain, as the British state grows more centralised. But London is losing influence in other ways: it is no longer the obvious cultural capital; its life-style and fashion are no longer imitated by provincials; innovation seems now to happen elsewhere in the islands and to reach London later. Its glamour has gone, and indeed all the Romes and Parises and other *villes-lumières* are growing dim. By contrast, the lights of Cardiff and Glasgow and Stuttgart and Lyon and Barcelona are growing brighter. The regionalist movement is, not least, a revival of big non-capital cities; they may not call themselves city-states, as Hamburg or Bremen do, but the powerful regions around them can be seen less as a "province" than as a city-state hinterland: what the Athenians used to call the *chora* of the *polis*.

This is a promising framework. Political diversity for regions and cities can enable "real", physical local diversity in small communities. I say "can", not "will"; when a political environment open to local initiatives has been achieved, it is still up to the taste and willpower of communities to seize their chance. They may equally well waste it. They may, for instance, find it baffling to say exactly what their distinctiveness is - or was.

That brings me to a final point. Once again, it is about the past and the assumption that local distinctiveness was long ago strong and is now slight.

This is almost certainly false. If you could travel through the villages of - say - Tudor Devon or East Sussex in the Plantagenet time, you would be appalled at their uniformity. The churches and manor houses would vary, though not nearly as much as they do now. But the cottages, the clothes, the carts and the fences would all look drably similar from one village to the next until you gradually crossed into the slightly different appearances of another county or district. And, outside the villages, it is hard to imagine how monotonous the pre-Enclosure landscape of England was. Anybody who has travelled through rural Russia or Hungary in the Communist period can understand a law of nature: poverty is the greatest enemy of local diversity.

In England, the diversity we are asked to treasure is seldom older than the 19th century. Then, really, began the rapid piling of one style on another, of this kind of shop rendered obsolete by a different kind of shop, of countless transient fashions in clothes and vehicles, in decoration and tools, in diet and song, of families migrating with their own accoutrements and customs from one region to another, finally of incomers reinventing what is supposed to be traditional but is in reality new. All leave survivals behind which build up into the bewildering, charming, rubbish-heap which we call diversity. I would like this process to continue, and indeed nobody can stop it now. But we should not give it a false pedigree.

Devon Is!
Edward Chorlton

Alphington, Ashcombe, Ashwater, Beer
Beaford, Berry Pomeroy, Bishopsteignton, Bow
Broadwoodwidger, Berrynarbor, Cheriton Fitzpaine
Clannaborough, Clovelly, Dunchideock, Eggesford ....

There are over 400 parishes in the County of Devon, each one is unique and distinct but they are all united by history, themes, threads and colours. Their residents can tell you about those matters, those corners, those issues and the folklore and culture that makes each parish and each part of that parish special to them. It may be folk knowledge about the Roman origin of a particular place only recently confirmed from a scientific point of view by aerial archaeology. It may be the history of the church, the school, its bridges or its nature. Equally it could be its bypass, its former traffic jams or its locally brewed beer. Devon to the resident, the 'local', the Devonian, is not necessarily the same Devon as that of the visitor or the recent 'incomer'. Martyn Brown in his "Red Guide-Devon" (1989) provides an interesting insight into visitor perception. He suggests that:

> The most popular image of Devon as a holiday destination is epitomised in the promotion of Torbay as the English Riviera; posters create an image of a sub-tropical paradise with perpetually blue skies and apparently warm seas but this image masks the tranquility and charm of much of the County and belies its rich variety.

> A contrasting view of the County might emphasise the fiery red soils of south-east Devon, matching the herds of Devon Red cattle, cider from a stoneware flask in an orchard of trees bent low under the heavy crop of fruit; black faced shaggy sheep seeking the shelter of roadside ditches; hedges plastered in primroses; and winters of deep snow that cut off farms for days on end.

These views are some way away from those of the idyllic photogenic paradise of the sepia photographs which were a feature of railway compartments and waiting rooms of the Great Western Railway. United by proximity to GWR stations these former images form a theme which can still be detected in Devon even where Beeching's infamous axe struck. One can only ask why BR do not similarly promote their destinations to create a wanderlust in their potential customers.

Various recent surveys have presented an interesting insight into what 'Devon Is' to the visitor. The things which scored highly with visitors to Devon were:
- a rich heritage
- a peaceful atmosphere
- lots to do/see
- good for off-peak
- good for the family
- clean beaches
- local people friendly
- beautiful scenery

The second survey looked at the visitor's perception of the quantitative and qualitative features of the County. These were:

(a)   *Quantitative* - Devon scored well on:
- beautiful, natural scenery
- places of interest and heritage sites to visit
- good touring area
- peaceful, quiet
- clean and well maintained
- historic towns

(b)   *Qualitative* - The main associations expressed were:
- holiday place
- nice beaches, fabulous coast
- caves, rock pools
- souvenir shops (horrible)
- nice countryside
- history
- moors
- tors
- small winding roads
- long walks
- country pubs/open fires
- "army camp" holiday parks
- farms, cows, sheep, fields
- little cottages
- quaint
- amusement arcades
- cream teas, clotted cream
- home made food
- Dartmoor prison
- sunshine
- people
- coastline
- retirement area

Many residents would add other features such as ports and harbours, thatched cottages, red soil, Devon hedgebanks, deep lanes, climate, Devon Red cattle, Dartmoor ponies, apples and cider orchards.

Devon's inheritance in terms of designation is illustrated below:

Designations
- 2 National Parks
- 4 Areas of Outstanding Natural Beauty (soon to be 5)
- 400 square miles of Area of Great Landscape Value
- 86 square miles of Coastal Preservation Area
- 5 stretches of Heritage Coast

International, national or local importance:-
- 12 Nature Conservation Zones
- approximately 200 Sites of Special Scientific Interest
- a Ramsar site and Special Protection Area (Exe Estuary)
- many other reserves and sites

Historic importance:-
- 250 Conservation Areas
- 22,000 listed buildings
- 100 Historic Settlements (21 of which are considered by the
  Council for British Archaeology to be of major historic
  importance)
- 1,000 Scheduled Ancient Monuments
- 43,000 entries on the Sites and Monuments Record
- 36 Historic Parks and Gardens

But how can a picture of 'real' Devon be presented? Geology and climate together with their resultant colours provide one thread; history, culture and folklore another; whilst a third is the unconformity created by contrasts between neighbouring settlements despite their similar origin or modern day function.

Throughout Europe geology and its related topography help to define a sense of place. Geology not only creates the landscape and its related wildlife habitats but more importantly it provides the local building materials. Its influence on soils and vegetation has historically determined the way in which an area is formed although today the common agricultural policy appears to have taken on this role with the countryside changing colours by turn from green, to yellow and to purple at the command of some cosmic artistic conductor in EC DG something.

Devon has a special place in the science of geology. Not only is it the site of at least one field trip for every UK geology student but it is the only county which gives its name to a geological era. The 'Devonian' system was defined in 1839 by the Reverend Adam Sedgewick and Sir Robert Murchison for those strata deposited after the Silurian slates and limestones of Wales and before the coal bearing strata of the Midlands.

Devon's geology is responsible for the County's characteristic red soils and red sea cliffs. Although the red rocks of Devon cover a considerable part of the County, this is still only a part of the whole. The characteristic 'red' image probably arises from railway routes into the County and along the coast in the Dawlish/Teignmouth area.

The tors of the granite heartland, the slates, gritstones, limestones, pebble beds and chalks all help to define what Devon is. Each of these has been exploited by local residents over hundreds of years to create a complexity of building styles and materials. Devon buildings look and feel distinctively Devonian because of their use of local Devon building materials, their plan forms and decorative details which were adopted to suit local conditions. No one building of the period 1400 to 1800 is exactly the same as another. Particularly notable features of Devon Buildings are shown below.

Cob walls - Irregular wall lines, thick walls, cob above stone plinths. Largely in middle and east Devon.
Thatch - Where other more permanent materials not available or too expensive. Distribution as above.
Slate - As a walling and roofing material in south, north and west.
Granite - As a walling material. Crude detailing, plain buildings, large boulders, only rarely ashlar.
Limestone - As a walling material in south. Easily cut to ashlar, sometimes polished in interior work. Creamy colour.
Sandstones - Have very wide variations in colours and textures in north east and south west.
Chert - A hard, flint like walling material, difficult to form corners and straight lines.
Volcanic Traps - Purple soft stone, easy to work but easily eroded.
Metamorphosed Tuff - Around Tavistock, a greenish rough stone easily cut.
Brick and Tile - Not common, largely in East Devon but by mid C19 more widely made
Timber - not a common material, most visible in C16 - C18 Town Houses.

One of the most interesting of these materials is cob. Cob is simply the Devon word for a mud wall. No other county in England has as much mud walling as Devon! Cob was used as the traditional means of mass wall construction throughout most of rural Devon during the period of the fourteenth to the nineteenth centuries.

The basic material was the on-site sub-soil. The cob was prepared by adding straw to the sub-soil, and the mixing process was often achieved by the treading of cattle whose dung provided a 'plasticiser' for the mixture. Cob itself varies from place to place as a result of local traditions and the widely differing nature of local sub-soils.

Devon's history has been influenced not just by its geology but also by its geographical place in the world. Whilst its parishes are all distinctly different to a large extent they have a common history and ancestry. Thought by some residents to be the most south-westerly county as the land beyond the Tamar defines itself as another country, Devon has no neighbours to the north and south except the Bristol and English Channels and is bounded to the east by the high ground of Exmoor and the Blackdowns.

Its situation has led to its fishing and international trading traditions. It has a long history of trading with North America, Northern Europe, the Iberian Peninsula and the Mediterranean. The farming, shipbuilding, quarrying and naval traditions which account for large parts of the population for many hundreds of years stem from Devon's peripheral but international position.

Whilst sailors and fishermen are known for their tall stories, folklore and myth are widespread in Devon. It is said that the devil has a richer heritage in Devon than many counties. On 8th February 1853, someone (or something) left a trail of footprints that covered 100 miles across the south of the County. Described as hooflike, and as that of a two-legged beast, they crossed fields, villages, walls and the roofs of houses. News spread to London, no doubt via the new railway, and articles appeared in The Times and the Illustrated London News!

During the evening of 5th November each year, the bell ringers of Shebbear in North Devon sound a discordant jangle on the bells of St. Michael's Church. Then, arming themselves with ropes and crowbars, they turn over a massive boulder which lies outside the eastern gate of the churchyard. If this is not done, they believe, some calamity will overtake Shebbear in the coming year. When the ceremony was omitted on one occasion during the First World War, the following 12 months brought misfortune to the village and its surrounding farms.

The boulder, a lump of quartz conglomerate six feet long and four feet wide and weighing almost a ton, is not geologically native to Shebbear. It was probably once used as the 'moot' or meeting stone of the Anglo-Saxon administrative 'Hundred' centred on Shebbear, but the stories surrounding it and its position due east of the church, beneath an ancient oak, suggest that it also figured in some pagan ritual. It was possibly in an attempt to neutralise the boulder's power that the early Christians of Shebbear decided to raise their church nearby, and to dedicate the building to St. Michael the Archangel, mightiest of all the Devil's opponents. If so, they were not entirely successful, for the Exeter Bishops' registers record that in 1454 the church was 'burnt by a fire from Hell': perhaps the stone had not turned that year!

Other stones especially older carved standing stones within or adjacent to the highway carry deeply held superstitions. Two such examples are 'Sidbury's Stone' and at Copplestone. Road designs have been adjusted to minimise or avoid the necessity to move these stones as their movement is said to result in a curse with potentially fatal results.

Superstition and tradition also govern the detail of the preparation of food and drink. Scrumpy cider is naturally fermented and not sweetened. Devonshire clotted cream the staple of a Devonshire Cream Tea has a commercial production history going back to the thirteenth century.

Clotted, or scalded cream is cream that has been heated. This helps to keep it longer than untreated cream, because heating destroys those bacteria that would otherwise turn the cream sour. Heating also gives the cream its distinctive flavour and thick granular texture. Four breeds of cattle found in Devon (Devon and North Devon, Guernsey and Jersey) all yield milk with a high butterfat content. Large fat globules rise quickly to form a thick layer of cream if the milk is allowed to stand undisturbed in the cool temperature of the dairy in large pans called 'setting pans'. Then the milk and cream are heated to a temperature of 77-78 degrees C for about 40 minutes and allowed to cool for up to 24 hours, depending on the weather. As the pans cool, a wrinkled crust forms which is skimmed off by hand. Devonshire cream is whiter and more runny than the yellower Cornish cream.

In the nineteenth century, Mrs. Beaton wrote: 'The cream is so much esteemed that it is sent to the London markets in small square tins and jars, and is exceedingly eaten with fresh fruit'. These traditions and history have created much of that which is most valued and distinctive in Devon today. This is both a rural and urban feature of the County. It is interesting to contrast adjacent towns and villages, Totnes and Newton Abbot in the south of the County and Topsham and Starcross located on opposite sides of the Exe estuary.

Totnes and Newton Abbot are both market towns, lying at the heads of tidal river systems and are settlements of considerable history. Although both have their origins several hundred years ago Totnes developed within its defensive walls whilst Newton Abbot was borne of the amalgamation of two manorial townships. Both are railway towns but whilst Totnes station serves the town with little impact on its development, Newton Abbot developed as a significant railway junction town. The railway set the foundations for the blossoming of Newton with the construction of a number of fine Victorian buildings and squares. Totnes has retained its medieval charm and is now a mecca for 'alternative cultures'.

Superficially Topsham and Starcross share many common characteristics - once small settlements on the Exe estuary, with a strong relationship with the river and linear development patterns.

Their history and building, however, reveal contrasting origins. Topsham goes back to Roman times with much development taking place in the 16th to 18th centuries. It retains its many small streets and alleys and in the Strand are to be found the attractive 'Dutch' houses built in the early 1700's, by the wool merchants. Dutch bricks were brought back from Holland as ballast and the design of the houses was clearly influenced by the Holland connection.

Starcross has humbler origins in the sixteenth century as a collection of fishermen's cottages. Brunel's atmospheric railway dominated the waterfront in the 19th century although a number of architecturally interesting buildings were constructed about the same time. The relatively recent demolition of the mental institution has created some space for the development of modern housing estates.

These contrasts, this history, these themes make it clear that in carrying out its statutory duties the County Council cannot properly maintain its stewardship of Devon without giving them proper recognition.

The Engineering and Planning Department (logo - a Luccombe Oak) is a multi-disciplinary department employing inter alia planners, engineers, ecologists, environmentalists, archaeologists, mathematicians, modellers, computer wizards, traffic specialists and listed building experts. Its responsibilities include the largest road network of any English County by far, planning, waste regulation, country parks, the environment, traffic and recycling. Its recently published Directory of Services details some 77 different services.

As an integrated department the protection and enhancement of both the rural and urban environment is a prime function. This ranges from landscape assessment on the one hand, through estuary management, and town enhancements to the protection of single lamp columns on the other.

Local Distinctiveness features strongly in the Department's Business Plan with reference to the need for all work of the department to recognise and respect the "little things" that make Devon what it is - "those little gems of local distinctiveness".

It is all too easy for technical staff to wish to 'standardise' its work to 'increase efficiency' and to increase the safety factor of its work. The safety issue is recognised. For example it is clearly necessary for standards to be consistent on long distance highway routes. This can, however, be achieved whilst still recognising or reading the landscape in which it should sit. Smaller schemes, smaller works, maintenance and enhancement works can and do ensure that changes recognise the importance of the cultural touchstones which describe and define our localities. Environmental as well as safety audits are carried out on schemes. Environmental Practice Guidelines cover issues such as landscape, nature conservation, the historic environment, and local distinctiveness.

The landscape checklist includes reference to matters such as geology, climate, energy and light. The local distinctiveness checklist includes:-

- Ensure that traditional building materials are used whenever possible
- Remember the importance people attach to places
- Try to identify the locally distinctive features of any area before preparing a highway scheme
- Adopt standards which are sympathetic to the character of an area
- Ensure that highway maintenance contributes to the overall enhancement of the local environment; where neglected or undertaken badly it detracts from the appearance of the area
- Pay special care and attention to all works in sensitive urban and rural areas, especially historic towns, conservation areas, National Parks and AONBs.

The approach is to recognise the identity of the places in which work is carried out whether it be major road schemes, a green tourism initiative such as the Tarka Trail or in the signing of rural roads.

Devon has adopted its own fingerpost system having reviewed and categorised its rural highway network. Each sign carries the distinctive Devon finial. Whenever a junction or crossroads has a locally accepted name this is included on the post. This not only helps to preserve the name but is also a valuable navigational aid.

Particular initiatives including grant aid have taken place, to help preserve particular habitats including Devon's orchards and Devon's own 'tropical rainforest' the Culm Grass Lands. Devon's verges policy, now 20 years old but having just had its fifth review, has set the standard nationally for roadside conservation. Conservation, thatching, archaeology, land management, eyesores and other grants all help to preserve the authenticity of Devon's environment. Training days have been held for staff to aid understanding and generate enthusiasm for the concept and philosophies described above.

Consultation with local communities and individuals is an essential part of all design and other initiatives. Working with the community in this way inspires, frustrates, provides enlightenment and aids lateral thinking. Preconceptions have to be left at home and the layers of local knowledge, history, colour and culture be recognised in all the Department's work. Whether it be

Oakford, Otterton, Petrockstowe, Poughill
Queens Nympton, Romansleigh, Shaldon, Tamerton Foliot
Upottery, Virginstowe, Woolfardisworthy, Woolfardisworthy (yes there are two), Yarcombe, Yeoford, Yelland or even Zeal Monachorum

then DEVON IS !

Bibliography
WG Hoskins *Devon*, Devon Books 1992
British Regional Geology *South West England*, HMSO 1993
Devon County Council *Devon Tourism Review 1992*, D.C.C. 1993
Devon County Council *Environmental Audit of Highway Schemes,*
D.C.C. 1993

Local Distinctiveness: an Idea for Europe
Michael Dower

During the last eight years, my work in ECOVAST[1] has taken me into 18 European countries, meeting people in the small towns, villages, and farms. I have gained a vivid impression of two impulses alive among these people:

- on the one hand, a commitment to Europe, a strong sense of our common heritage, of the historic flows and modern links between us

- on the other hand, a fierce pride in their particular place.

These impressions have strongly reinforced my own commitment to the idea of Europe and to the idea of local distinctiveness.

I am no expert on the geography or history of Europe. But much travel and much talk have given me a strong sense of the cultural links between different parts of Europe, springing from the long history of settlement, trade, the rise and fall of empires, the movements of people, the pursuit of religion and of learning. Roman amphi-theatres in France and Britain, Arab architecture in Spain, daughter monasteries of the great Abbey of Cluny in a dozen countries, Saxon folk in Transylvanian villages - these speak of the great movements of people and of ideas across the face of Europe.

These historic links, together with the relative compactness of this continent, give a sense of a European identity. Yet Europe is so intricate, so varied in climate, land form and geology, and so long settled that it contains a wonderful diversity of peoples and places.

The counterpoint between these two ideas - of Europe and of localness - came home to me when I became a Conseilleur d'Honneur de la Connetablie de Guyenne, at Blaye, north of Bordeaux. This constabulary was set up in medieval times, when English Kings were the Dukes of Aquitaine. Now it is revived as a confrerie of winegrowers: to them I swore that I would defend the good name of the wines of Blaye and of Bourg, whose distinctive local quality the guild now protects.

Local distinctiveness is seen, by many people throughout Europe, as a precious asset at a time when all parts of the continent are affected by processes which threaten that distinctiveness. These forces, often originating outside the continent, are the modern equivalents of the imperialism of Rome or the great eastward spread of German culture in the middle ages. They include:

- the centralising of political and economic policies, notably within the European Economic Community, which is itself set to expand north and east over the coming years;

- the growth of multi-national companies, with bases in Europe or in America, Japan or elsewhere, whose aim is to secure a large share of the European or world market in their sector of commerce, often with standardised products;

- the growing domination of popular culture in Europe by films, music and other media aimed at mass appeal, with a very strong element of American origin; and

- the growing domination by the English, Spanish and French languages.

I had a hint of the strength of these forces when I went into a hardware shop in a small town in eastern Croatia, seeking a battery for my Japanese camera. I could see no staff, till a noise at the far end of the store revealed them all clustered in a corner, watching Dallas on television!

These standardising forces are having a powerful impact in Europe, particularly among young people. But there is also a strong desire, among millions of Europeans, to retain what is local and special alongside what is standardised and universal.

Few Europeans wish to deny the benefits of cheap, mass-produced products which meet essential needs with minimum drudgery. These goods are being eagerly sought by the people of central Europe, as they emerge from their 45 lost years. But in a threatening, uncertain world, there is a strong impulse to seek shelter and support among the familiar and the local. It is as if people seek a two-speed life...high tech and low tech...universal and local...standardised and distinctive.

How is this impulse to local distinctiveness expressed in Europe? Let me answer this by use of the three key words used by that great pioneer, Patrick Geddes, who did so much to encourage the understanding of place in the early part of this century. His trilogy was 'folk, work and place'.

Folk

Geddes used the word 'folk' in no twee sense. His focus was on people, their language, custom and culture, their way of life. In these respects, Europe offers rich diversity still, and a high measure of local distinctiveness.

The Europe of some three dozen nation-states may be striving towards a greater measure of political and economic union. Yet it contains a vastly greater number of entities, in each of which the people feel some special bond of ethnic origin, religion, language, dialect or culture which sets them apart from others and which they wish to sustain and express in their daily lives.

Consider France, that most centralised of western European countries. Think of the pride of the Gascons, the Bretons, the Alsaciens...and how that pride is expressed in dialect, in food, in dance and dress. How the girls of Britanny vie each year to become queen of their town! How the young men step the traditional dance to the tune of the bombard!

Governments in Europe are obliged to recognise these loyalties, at least at regional level. In some countries, such as Germany and Italy, the regions have a strong administrative and cultural role. The European Commission looks increasingly to the Europe of the Regions. But in many countries there is tension between the centre and the regions, which has surfaced in independence movements, and (in some places) arson, terrorism and civil strife: think of Scotland, Wales, the Basque country, the Walloon and Flemish people in Belgium, or the recently-gained independence of Slovenia and Croatia. A deeper element of tragedy is added where two or more ethnic or religious groups compete for regional identity over a single territory, as in Cyprus, Northern Ireland or Bosnia-Herzegovina.

Against these tensions and tragedies may be set the continued vitality of distinctive cultures within, and sometimes crossing the boundaries of, our nation-states. Think, for example, of the Sami people, only some 50,000 in total, who pursue their part-settled, part-nomadic way of life, dependent on the reindeer, across a swathe of country in Norway, Sweden, Finland and Russia. They keep their own language, culture, dress, and customs; and have recently harnessed telecommunications to the cause of their decentralised life.

But our concern is with something more subtle, more innate to daily life, than broad regional character and loyalties - namely the local distinctiveness which makes each small community, each parish or neighbourhood, special. Governments are generally not good at nurturing local distinctiveness. Their national, and even their regional, administrations tend to apply standardised, top-down policies to places with widely different character and needs. Reform of local government, as in Germany and in Britain, has enlarged the local authority areas and removed the 'town hall' from many towns. France with its 36,000 communes, or Luxembourg with only two tiers of government, may be better placed to articulate and to meet local needs.

More deadly than the enlarging of local authorities is the centralising of power or economic activity within a nation. These forces can sap the energy of local communities, particularly those whose youth or menfolk move away in search of work. Local pride can then turn into the apathy and impotence which now blight significant parts of rural France, Portugal, Spain, Italy and the countries of central Europe.

But local pride is a tough instinct. It can lie dormant through drought; and then revive when irrigated. Patrick Geddes recognised this, when he animated the folk in the run down tenements of Edinburgh or (later) the untouchables in the villages of India. Others, today, are acting in the same spirit.

I offer a striking example from western Poland. Two brothers, Bogdan and Witold Chmielewski, professors of art at the University of Torun, 15 years ago bought and restored a derelict hunting-lodge. They came to know the people of the nearby village of Lucim, a parish of less than 300 souls which had lost all state-recognised function other than its state farm and forest. Its people were poor and demoralised, its economy limited, its fabric deteriorating.

The brothers Chmielewski encouraged the revival of the traditional festivals - Christmas, Easter, mid-summer, Michaelmas. Under their guidance, the people researched the history of the village; discovered that it was founded in 1459; recorded the local events of the last 500 years, by reference to their own families; took the festival events out into each corner of the parish...and, in the process, revived their latent local pride. Five years ago, their courage was so refreshed that they decided to build a cultural centre, equal in size and quality to the best of English village halls. That centre is due to open this summer; and the people are now aiming to create other facilities and to strengthen the economy of the parish.

Work
Much of the rich diversity of Europe has arisen from the different ways in which men and women have worked - with the raw materials that were to hand - to create food, clothing and shelter and to meet their other needs.

This work, over many human generations, has shaped both land and people; and the variety of natural resources in Europe has combined with the ethnic variety of the people to create astonishing diversity. Local distinctiveness has been created by the patterns of hunting, forestry, farming, quarrying, building, production of tools and clothing and food.

This distinctiveness is expressed in the local economy, the skills of the people, their language, their pride, their artifacts, even their very appearance and physique. I remember the shock of seeing photographs of the bare feet of the people who, until the 1930's, lived on the remote island of St Kilda. Their diet was based on the eggs of sea-birds, to get which they swung down ropes from the cliff-top, gripping the cliff with feet clad only in socks, gaining a breadth and strength in their toes unique to that place.

I do not wish to idealise the traditional working practices of (say) the last century, when many millions in Europe faced lives of toil and hardship. But I record with regret that the rich diversity of most local economies has been much reduced by the industrial revolution and the centralising forces of capitalism or communism. The replacement of the horse by the tractor, of hand-made bricks and tiles by mass-produced roofing materials, of local beers by Heineken (reaching parts which others used to serve!) has made life easier for many but also vitiated the character and weakened the economy of thousands of localities.

A counter-attack is now well under way: the aim is not to try to halt the powerful process of mass-production or the growth of multi-national companies, but rather to revive and strengthen local economies throughout Europe. This counter-attack is based upon (among other things) the growing demand for purer food, for regional food products, for hand-made goods, and for rural tourism. As their incomes rise, people are prepared to buy honey from a named location rather than a blend "from the sunny countries of the world"; farm-fresh food rather than supermarket vegetables; pottery with a distinct local character.

Prince Charles attracted wide support when he protested at the European Commission's hygiene rules which threatened the closure of the small family firms who produce speciality cheeses such as the French Brie de Meaux or Bleu d'Auvergne. He and other protestors secured the reprieve of these cheeses. In this country, local specialities such as Craster Kippers or Devon Clotted Cream are hanging on under threat from the hygiene rules.

It is ironic that this is the same EC that has funded the LEDA initiative, for local economic development. This has encouraged (for example) the revival of traditional pottery and embroidery in the community of Nisa, Portugal, and the forming of marketing cooperatives through which the salmon farmers of western Ireland sell fish to Paris and the wine-growers of Sitia in Crete sell their wine in Munich. In many other areas, efforts are being made by cooperatives, syndicats d'initiatives, local authorities, enterprise agencies and governments to promote local products.

Powerful assistance to the cause of strengthening local economies can come from two modern forces which may appear to be part of the anti-local process of our society - namely tourism, and information technology.

Tourism is progressively penetrating Europe, as people seek new places to visit and local authorities strive to create jobs. If ill-managed, tourism can shatter the culture and distort the economy of a place. If well-managed, it can reinforce the existing economy and help to sustain the livelihoods and character of the place. Tourists who visit rural areas tend to look for what is special about that place, and their money may help to sustain such features. That is why ECOVAST has been helping to promote rural tourism throughout Europe, particularly in Hungary, Slovakia and adjoining countries with their weak economy and remarkable heritage. It is why, for example, we see tourism as a key part of the proposal for a Regional Park in the inland part of Istria, that beautiful peninsula in western Croatia whose hinterland has lost its earlier vitality as people moved away to work on the coast.

Information technology can be seen as a powerful force for cultural standardisation, fuelled by competition between multi-national companies. But it is also a remarkable liberator, permitting people everywhere to overcome the disadvantages of sparse population, distance, and even social isolation and physical handicap. It can enable people to work where they want to live, firms to market their local products more widely, local shops and other services to remain viable...all positive effects in protecting local distinctiveness. That is why ECOVAST has been working to encourage the creation of telecottages and the spread of teleworking.

Place

The third part of Geddes' trilogy is place - the look and feel of the land, shaped and coloured in each locality by the particular combination between nature and human use.

There is a strong human instinct to set roots in a place, to stay in or return to the place of one's ancestors. This yearning forms a main theme in the folk songs of Europe, such as those written by emigrants from Ireland. Homesickness is often prompted, not by a dramatic landscape or a distant view, but by the intimate detail of a place - a bend in the lane, a familiar street or group of trees, the noise of nesting rooks or the smell of horses.

The love which people bear for a place is often unconscious. It grows on them and becomes part of their being, but may remain unspoken...until there comes a threat to the place, whereupon people often react strongly in defence of what they love. We should not deride such reactions to change. But we should recognise that the love of place which prompts resistance to change is often associated with baser instincts, such as protection of privilege or of property values.

The counterpoint to this, among those who do not have privilege or valuable property, and who may indeed be in dire poverty, maybe a positive desire for change, of a type which may strike the outside observer as doing grave damage to local distinctiveness. I think, for example, of the rash of cement-block bungalows along the western coast of Ireland; of the mini-villas, of cheap brick and concrete tile, built by returning migrant workers in the mediaeval granite villages of Portugal; or of new corrugated iron flashing among the shingle roofs of Slovenian timber houses.

We who care for the sustaining of local distinctiveness must face this hard dilemma. Distinctiveness cannot be protected despite the wishes of the local people. Rather, it must be protected for the people, and by them. This will only happen if they see that it is in their interest to protect it...and that requires that a balance and mutual support be found between folk and work and place.

This mutual support between people and place forms the underlying theme of ECOVAST's work in rural Europe. It is also a theme on which we in Britain have strong practical experience to offer to our fellow Europeans. Think of the schemes through which payments are offered to farmers to sustain those traditional farming practices which created and which can protect special features of the landscape such as flower-rich meadows and orchards; the woodland management schemes which produce usable products and sustain wildlife, landscape and recreation; and the projects to restore historic buildings and thereby to provide affordable housing or workshops.

ECOVAST is promoting practical approaches of these kinds throughout Europe. Our Rural Architecture Group, for example, brings together a widespread network of enthusiasts who are striving to protect, and where necessary to put to appropriate new use, buildings of traditional local character.

Such action must involve those who own or occupy those buildings. But it very often demands also funds, expertise and even materials from outside the locality. Consider, for example, the great continuing tradition of timber building in Sweden, including the painted farmhouses and barns. The deep red Falun paint comes from a single source, the great copper mine at Stora Kopparberg. Advice and raw materials for the repair of historic timber houses is offered by the Centre for Old Buildings at Gysuge Brok. Without these two crucial sources the local tradition would gradually wither.

I conclude by thanking Common Ground for initiating this Conference. I hope that it will stimulate thinking and action about local distinctiveness in this country and elsewhere in Europe. ECOVAST will be happy to help.

1. ECOVAST: the European Council for the Village and Small Town was set up in 1984 to further the well being of rural communities and the safeguarding of the rural heritage throughout Europe. It has a network of over 300 members across East and West Europe including over 80 organisations including government and non government organisations from local to international.

The Apple, the Orchard, the Cultural Landscape.

Angela King and Sue Clifford

The apple is a wonderful symbol of variety, the orchard an intricate example of the cultural landscape.

In Britain we have grown 6,000 varieties of apples, hundreds more cider apples, and hundreds of pears, plums, damsons, cherries and nuts. Many of these are traceable to their place of origin. The Bramley apple was grown from a pip by Mary Ann Brailsford 190 years ago in Southwell, Nottinghamshire, it is still there; Mr Hale of Swanpool raised the Worcester Pearmain. Some were simply found, such as the Victoria plum discovered in a wood in Sussex and the Newton Wonder (it is said) in the thatched roof of the Hardinge Arms pub in King's Newton, Derbyshire.

This link with place may be so particular that the variety will only grow, or produce tasty fruit within a short distance. Apple trees, like most plants, are adapted to local conditions and do best where they originated. Coul Blush, Britain's most northerly (surviving) apple variety hails from Easter Ross and does well in northern and exposed situations, whereas D'Arcy Spice prefers the dryer, warmer summers of Essex and the south east. Apples are often named after the place they came from - Alfriston, Crawley Beauty, Cambusnethan Pippin, Carlisle Codlin, or by the person who raised them - Cox, Laxton, Charles Ross, John Standish.

When we started the Save our Orchards campaign in 1988, old orchards had few champions. They had fallen between the stools of agriculture and conservation. Horticulture has never enjoyed the attention that farming has, and environmentalists have rarely considered cultivated trees or orchards to be within their ambit, even though they can be rich habitats for wild life.

Orchards are more than formal collections of fruit trees, they are a manifestation of our long relationship with fruit cultivation in different localities. They vary from place to place in the kind of fruit, the varieties, size and disposition of trees, the domestic animals that are grazed beneath them, the soft fruits, flowers and other crops grown around them, the ways and times of pruning, grafting, picking and packing.

Current gardening and agricultural practice encourages us to believe that we can and should grow almost anything anywhere. And yet we know that plants tend to grow better where the conditions for them occur naturally and that trees make places as much as buildings or the underlying geology.

Until the 1950's orchards were widespread throughout the British Isles. Almost every farm had its orchard. In the last thirty years the total orchard area has declined by two thirds - around 150,000 acres have been lost. In Devon, almost 90% of their orchards have disappeared since 1965. There are many factors - local, national and international - which have contributed to the demise of commercial orchards and the small garden and farm orchards used for domestic consumption.

Nineteenth century legislation stopped payment in kind to farm labourers (farm cider had long been a cheap way of remunerating workers); the commercial production of artificial pectin sounded the death-knell for those orchards of Yorkshire which produced apples to set Rowntree's fruit gums; the substitution of the orange for the vitamin C-rich apple for sailors against scurvy must have decimated orchards accessible to ports; the standardization which has followed the attempt to set standards for shape/colour/size/robustness of fruit has led to many varieties being dropped; an increasing belief in scientific progress has sacrificed much local wisdom; competition from cheap imported apple concentrates for cider production and the successful advertising and marketing of apples from other continents needs no elaboration.

Added to this has been a peculiar devaluing of local produce. Instead of being a matter of pride, we have been so seduced by international cuisine and produce that it has been more important for the supermarket to sell chillies or strawberries out of season from the USA, at the expense of seasonal local vegetables, fruit, cheese or meat. Our orchards should be as important to us as vineyards are to the French or olive groves to the Greeks.

Soils, aspect, climate and culture play an important part in the distribution of types of fruit and of different varieties. For example, the south-facing well-drained rain-washed slopes of the south Devonshire valleys are ideal for growing cider apples. The shallow stony soils on the Kentish Ragstone produce the best cobnuts.

The Blaisdon Red plum is reputed to 'flourish with the health and vigour of a weed' in the five mile radius of Blaisdon in west Gloucestershire, 'but with few exceptions it does not thrive elsewhere'. Other types of plums were particular to place - the Aylesbury Prune, the Bryanston Gage, the Cambridge Gage,

Dittisham Ploughman, Dymock Plum, Farleigh Damson, Landkey Yellow, Pershore Yellow Egg and Warwickshire Drooper. The hedgerows of Shropshire are dotted with damsons, linear orchards, some grown originally for the dyeing of Lancashire cloth.

Fruit trees present us with a never ending potential for variety since the seeds do not grow true. But many of the resulting offspring are not to our liking. Over the centuries, from the millions of possibilities, we have selected as useful and grown a few thousand varieties. Around our orchard fruit have grown particular recipes, drinks, songs, poetry, folklore and customs. Continuity is obviously crucial to the development of people's relationship with the land and its harvest.

In Gloucestershire alone, there are about 100 perry pear varieties worthy of note, and each parish or district would have produced its own characteristic single variety perry.

Should we try to hold on to those magnificent Gloucestershire perry pear orchards, the 60 foot high cherry groves of north Kent or the mossy cider orchards of Devon and Somerset? Are there reasons beyond commerce to maintain them?

When you lose an orchard you sacrifice not simply a few old trees (bad enough, some would say) but you might lose for ever varieties particular to that locality, the wild life, the songs, the recipes, the cider/perry/cherry brandy, the hard but social work, the festive gatherings, the look of the landscape, the wisdom gathered over generations about pruning and grafting, about aspect and slope, soil and season, variety and use. In short the cultural landscape is diminished by many dimensions at one blow.

Museum-like gatherings of varieties in one place are vulnerable to disease and the knowledge of scientists is different from vernacular understanding. We need both. Particularly we need to value and keep wisdom in place.

Consider how the arguments are developing in other parts of the world; the Kpelle people of Liberia 'carefully match crop strains with the slope, soil conditions and sunlight conditions on each patch of their land. Women of the forest dwelling Kpelle sow more than 100 varieties of rice, making their fields a jigsaw of genetic diversity' (Dunning). Compare this with the wisdom of our local orchard growers.

We believe the viability of the orchard is linked with ours. The potential which they embody, in terms of genetic diversity is important, just as the knowledge of exactly where they grow best, what seasons will produce what quantities, how to prune and reproduce best from them, what are their qualities of keeping, cooking and production.

Sheep, pigs, and fowls were all associated with these places. The Gloucester Old Spot tastes better if it has been grazed in an orchard. Chickens eat codlin moth and fruit fly larvae. Multiple use can offer a self correcting system.

We should value orchards more and should seek new uses for them. Take the 60 foot tall remnant cherry orchards around Teynham and Faversham in Kent. These places, breathtaking at blossom time, used as a back-drop for garden furniture in expensive glossy magazines, are not valued as cultural landscapes. No one has thought that visitors might find them beautiful as camping sites, for walking and picnics, as open air restaurants, or good for orchard egg production, and other uses for the 21st century. Their potential lies, as does much of agriculture now, in multi-purpose use and adding value to the crops within the farm or community.

Traditional orchards will continue to provide an important bank of fruits and knowledge for a time when local produce and varieties will be valued in new contexts. They will maintain identity and authenticity, and keep intricate local expertise and cultural connections alive.

Common Ground has done a great deal of work to promote the conservation of old orchards and to plant new ones. Through books, pamphlets, exhibitions, articles, work through the media and collaborations we have drawn attention to the large numbers of apple varieties (and other fruits) found and raised in this country. We have started a county gazetteer of varieties to encourage people to grow fruits that are particularly associated with their own localities and are about to produce an Apple Map of Britain.

In 1990 we initiated Apple Day, on October 21 in Covent Garden, bringing fruit back for the first time in 17 years. Our intention was to demonstrate that with few resources and people a real celebration and exposition can be organised which can change things. We displayed over 100 varieties of apples which had been sent to us by enthusiasts from all over the country. These held a special fascination for people. So many different shapes, sizes and colours. The evocative names, the smells. Tastings were very popular, and memories of childhood orchards and almost forgotten names came pouring out. People with anonymous apple trees in their gardens came back clutching glorious collections of fruit hoping to have them identified.

Our intentions were never to do it again ourselves, but rather to establish a new day in the calendar, an annual festival, a popular widening of interest and commitment leading to the revitalising of the orchards themselves. Linking the apple we eat with the landscape around us is a way of building responsibility back into our own actions.

In 1991 we launched Apple Day countrywide and intend to continue to promote it over several years to help consolidate and extend the idea.

The appeal and the potential is very great, already in its second year Apple Day 1992 was celebrated in over 80 places organised by County and District Councils from Cornwall to Ryedale, schools, village halls, the National Trust, museums, juice producers, apple growers, cider makers, farmers, nurserymen, bakers, restaurants, wildlife trusts, supermarkets, arts centres, agricultural and horticultural colleges, the Houses of Parliament and the school meals service of North Yorkshire.

Celebration can be organized at the local level by anyone with the interest and energy to do it. Everything from apple suppers at home to grand gatherings in stately houses, pruning and grafting demonstrations, apple expositions and identification, apple bobbing and poetry readings.

Common Ground has also been promoting the idea of community orchards, school orchards and city orchards, ways of rethinking what these places could be for, who could benefit and take responsibility for them.

We worked on a model project with the Colne Valley Park Groundwork Trust and local people to create a community orchard in Colnbrook where in the 1820's Richard Cox had raised what was to become known as the Cox's Orange Pippin. We commissioned the sculptor/blacksmith Richard Farrington to make three metal seats which spell the word C O X and to stamp on them stories about the apple. These form tree guards as well as seats, and when the trees are bigger will be useful for helping yourself to the fruit. Colnbrook had virtually forgotten its role in this historic creation, an apple now grown in many parts of the world and worth more than £80 million to our national economy. As travellers look down on this little place from just beyond Heathrow's runways and others deliberate Colnbrook's future in Berkshire, its present in Surrey and its past in Middlesex, this small orchard reinforces something of the identity of the place, a quiet reminder of continuity and connectedness.

Many school, community and city orchards are being conserved or developed. Within the Groundwork Trusts alone, in celebration of the anniversary of the

Queen's Accession, 63 new orchards were planted in 1992, most with local or royal varieties.

The Countryside Commission has added orchards to its Countryside Stewardship grant system. Research has been commissioned in northern England and in Wales. Following the pioneering work of Somerset, other County Councils such as Cornwall, Devon, Hereford and Worcester and Kent are among the County Councils now giving grants or advice.

The North Devon Trust has created a network of people in their locality who support each other and share their knowledge. Safeway, Sainsbury's, Marks and Spencer would all acknowledge the importance of our campaigning, we await their autumn list of varieties to see whether or not they will maintain their aspirations to widen the range of English apples in season. Local people and groups have generated parish maps of local fruit varieties, worked with local authorities and farmers to make community orchards, schools have planted orchards, people have rediscovered varieties thought to be extinct and recipes, songs and celebrations have been revived. Food lobbyists have asked if they can build on our work. Tasmania is contemplating holding Apple Day next year and contact with various European groups is growing.

Orchards are a wonderful example of variety and culture and place - of local distinctiveness. Essentially we have established a popular project on genetic diversity crucially linked with the importance of keeping knowledge and practice alive in their place (which is real sustainablility), without frightening people. We have demonstrated that people know a lot, care deeply and are willing to do something about it.

References
Orchards a guide to local conservation   Common Ground 1989
Alan Dunning quoted in *United Nations Development Programme: Choices*
Vol 2 No 2 1993

The Contributors

Neal Ascherson is a journalist and author. Since 1990 he has been a columnist for The Independent on Sunday. He has written for The Observer, The Scotsman and The Manchester Guardian. He was Reporter of the Year 1982, Journalist of the Year 1987, and received the James Cameron Award in 1989. His books include: 'The Struggles for Poland' and 'Games with Shadows'.

Edward Chorlton is the County Engineer and Planning Officer for Devon. His responsibilities include planning, archaeology, listed buildings, public rights of way, transportation, road and bridge design and traffic calming. He sees one of his prime roles as bringing together all the professionals in his Department to help improve the quality of life whilst resolving conflicts and protecting all that is precious and distinctive in Devon.

Sue Clifford a founder director of Common Ground is now joint co-ordinator, she has worked in landscape and planning consultancies in Scotland, and as a lecturer in the Polytechnic of Central London and in University College London in the Bartlett School of Architecture and Planning. Throughout the 1970s she did pioneering work on environmental impact analysis and was on the Board of Directors of Friends of the Earth . Her books with Angela King include: 'Trees be Company - an anthology of poetry about trees'.

Gillian Darley is an architectural writer, currently for The Observer. Among her books are 'Villages of Vision' a study of the planned village in all its forms from the utopian to the expedient; 'Built in Britain', for the Channel 4 series celebrating the local nature of traditional building; and a biography of Octavia Hill. She is vice chairwoman of S.P.A.B. 1991-93.

Roger Deakin is a writer and film-maker. Formerly he was an advertising creative director, an English and drama teacher, creative consultant to Friends of the Earth and jazz and folk music advisor to the Aldeburgh Foundation. He is a member of the Eastern Arts Board General and Community Arts Panel. He is a founder director of Common Ground and with Angela King and Sue Clifford edited PULP! the newspaper all about trees.

Michael Dower is past President, and currently Vice President of ECOVAST, the European Council for the Village and Small Town, a pan-European network committed to the well-being of local communities and of the natural and cultural heritage through rural Europe. He is the Director General of the Countryside Commission, and was previously the National Park Officer of the Peak National Park, Director of the Dartington Institute and a planner with London County Council.

Angela King is a founder director and has worked for Common Ground since 1983. She is now joint co-ordinator. In the early 1970s she was Friends of the Earth's first wild life campaigner, initiating the groundbreaking campaigns for whales, big cats, otters and other endangered species, later working on habitat loss for Earth Resources Research and the Nature Conservancy Council. Her books with Sue Clifford include: 'Holding Your Ground - an action guide to local conservation'.

Richard Mabey is an acclaimed writer and broadcaster on our relations with nature. Author of 'The Common Ground'. and 'Gilbert White - a biography' (which won the Whitbread Biography Award in 1986). He is currently working on a cultural flora of Britain ' Flora Britannica' in collaboration with Common Ground, to be published by Sinclair Stevenson in 1995. He is active in grass-roots conservation and 'owns' a community woodland near his home in the Chilterns.

Patrick Wright is a writer and broadcaster. His first book, 'On Living in an Old Country' is widely credited with having created a new understanding of the heritage industry. He co-authored 'Recording Britain' which accompanied the exhibition at the V & A. His most recent book is 'A Journey Through Ruins'. He has written for Modern Painters, The London Review of Books, New Statesman & Society, The Observer, The Independent on Sunday and now writes regularly on varied cultural matters for The Guardian.

Common Ground Rules
for
Local Distinctiveness

Fight for AUTHENTICITY *and integrity. Keep places lived in, worked in and real. Demand the* BEST *of the new.*

Value the COMMON *place. Our Cultural Landscapes are our ordinary history and everyday nature intertwined.*

CHANGE *things for the better. Not for the sake of it! !*

Let the CHARACTER *of the people and place express itself. Kill corporate identity before it kills our high streets. Give local shops precedence.*

Defend DETAIL. *Respond to the local and the vernacular. No new building or development need be bland, boring or brash.*

Local DIALECT *should be spoken, heard and seen.*

ENHANCE *the natural features - rivers and brooks, hills and valleys, woods and heaths. Never let a stream be culverted: out of sight and open to abuse.*

We need ENCHANTMENT, *clear streams as well as clean water in our daily lives.*

Take the place's FINGERPRINT. *Forget words such as resource, site, customers and the public. Abstractions lead us astray. Think and talk about places and people.*

Get to know your GHOSTS. *The hidden and unseen stories and legends are as important as the visible.*

Don't fossilize places. HISTORY *is a continuing process, not just the past. Celebrate time, place and the seasons with Feasts and Festivals.*

Our IMAGINATION *needs diversity and variegation. We need standards not standardisation.*

Work for local IDENTITY. *Oppose monoculture in our fields, parks, gardens and buildings. Resist formulae and automatic ordering from pattern books which homogenise and deplete.*

JETTISON *your car whenever you can and go by public transport. Places are for people and nature not cars. Cars can detach us from places and unwittingly allow their destruction.*

Know your place. Facts and surveys are not the same as KNOWLEDGE *and wisdom. Itinerant expertise needs to meet with aboriginal, place based knowledge so we can make the best of both worlds.*

Buy things that are LOCALLY DISTINCTIVE *and locally made - such as food and souvenirs. Resist the things that can be found anywhere.*

The LAND *is sacred in many cultures. Why have we put a protective noose around the spectacular and the special and left the rest? All of our surroundings are important to someone.*

Places carry MEANING *in their associations and symbolisms. Don't plough through significance, it cannot be recreated. The well or tree may be the reason why a place is where it is.*

Bring the countryside to the town. Keep the fruit, vegetable and local produce MARKETS *open and alive. We should be able to buy Norfolk Biffins in Norwich and James Grieves in Edinburgh.*

NAMES *carry resonances and secrets. Respect local names and add new ones with care. It is not good enough to call a new estate 'Badger's Mead' when the badgers have been destroyed.*

Let NATURE *in. Encourage the plants that want to grow in your locality. You'll find a succession of good and diverse neighbours that bring richness to your doorstep.*

Champion the ORDINARY *and everyday.*

Get to know your place intimately. Search out PARTICULARITY & PATINA *help add new layers of interest.*

QUALITY *cannot by quantified. You know when something is important to you - make subjective and emotional arguments. Don't be put off because the professionals have marginalised all the things they can't count. Make them listen and look.*

REVEAL *the geology. Use the brick and stone of the locality. Reinforce the colour, patterns, craftsmanship and work of the place.*

REMEMBER *the depth of people's attachment to places. Do not undermine local pride and rootedness with insensitive change.*

REVEAL *the past! Decay is an important process. Don't tidy things up so much that the layers of history and reclamation by nature are obliterated. Let continuity show.*

Personality often resides in SUBTLETY *and idiosyncrasy. Look closely and often.*

Get things in proportion and in SCALE. *Every place has its own distinctive dimensions.*

THWART *the urbanization of the countryside. Fight the kerbstones and other roadside paraphernalia.*

USE *old buildings again. Find new functions for them. Accretion is better than demolition.*

VALUE *your own values! Democracy thrives on discussion about things that matter to us. Let the experts in on your terms.*

Slow down, wisdom comes through WALKING, *talking and listening.*

Exile XENOPHOBIA *which fossilizes places and peoples. Welcome cultural diversity and vive la différence.*

Make an alphabet of YOUR *own place. Work to reinforce local distinctiveness. Play your part, celebrate your differences.*

Y FILLTIR SGWAR - *that place which you own through familiarity and which 'owns' you needs your vigilance.*

Introduce ZEITGEIST *to genius loci. Don't let the signs of the times destroy the power of the place.*

ZONING *and segregation kill places! ! If industry is bad enough to be hidden should it exist at all?*

From Common Ground's Broadsheet May Day 1992.

Common Ground

Common Ground is working to encourage new ways of looking at the world to excite people into remembering the richness of the common place and the value of the everyday, to savour the symbolisms with which we have endowed nature, to revalue our emotional engagement with places and all that they mean to us, and to go on to become actively involved in their care.

We have chosen to focus attention not singularly on natural history or architecture or art or social history or legend or literature but on their complex combining which is the reality of people's relationship with their places, and which begins in our hearts but gets mediated by reason.

In attempting to reassert the importance of liberating our subjective response to the world about us we often turn for philosophical help to those who wear their emotions on their sleeve. We work with people from all branches of the arts. Much of what we do attempts to place cultural arguments and evidence beside the scientific, technical and economic rationales which so dominate and often debilitate our ways of thinking and doing.

Working through model projects and events and publications which provide direct information for direct action, our philosophy asserts that while conservation arguments remain solely in the scientific constituency (ecology, economics, etc) they remain partial and flawed. As they gravitate towards the cultural arena they return to deep concerns about our ethical relations with nature, about our ancient understanding of the land, about symbolism and stories that place us actively but benignly within the world. And it is our ordinary actions which will be our salvation or our downfall.

Common Ground is a small charity, formed in 1983, funded by government agencies, charitable trusts, business and donations.

We do not have branches or a membership. We inspire and encourage people to become actively involved in their own places - rather than giving us money to do it for them.

Some Common Ground Publications

Common Ground Rules for Local Distinctiveness - an ABC of the locally particular from Ayrshire Cows to Zennor church (illustrated broadsheet, colour, A2) £4.50.

Local Distinctiveness leaflet (single copies free with sae)

Holding Your Ground - an action guide to local conservation, Angela King and Sue Clifford, Wildwood House, 1987 £8.95.

Orchards - a guide to local conservation, Common Ground, 1989 £6.00.

The Apple Source Book, particular recipes for diverse apples, (contributors include: Michael Barry, Elizabeth David, Sophie Grigson, Roy Lancaster, Prue Leith & Joan Morgan), Common Ground, 1991 £5.70.

Apple Map of Britain - showing where particular apples come from, their history, stories, uses, recipes, drinks, cultivation. (A1, full colour) £6.00.

Parish Maps, Tom Greeves, Common Ground, 1987 £1.75.

New Milestones: Sculpture, Community and the Land, Joanna Morland, Common Ground, 1988 £6.00.

Sculpture and the land, set of 4 black & white postcards of works by Andy Goldsworthy, Alain Ayers, Peter Randall-Page and John Maine, 50p each or £2.40 for set of 4.

Places: the City and the Invisible, Sue Clifford, Public Art Development Trust, 1993

Mayday, Mayday: 101 Ways to answer Nature's Call for help (A2, broadsheet), Common Ground, 1988 £3.50.

Festival Cards, six large-format postcards which celebrate 4 ancient & 2 new festivals. Full colour set or specify your own mix of 6 £5.00.

Tree Dressing Day Times - 8 page tabloid newspaper giving reports and ideas on Tree Dressing celebrations. 50p + A4 sae

Tree Dressing Day - poster full of 100s of beautiful drawings,lots of ideas, (A1, full colour), £5.50.

Apple Day, Save our Orchards, Community Orchards, Tree Dressing Day and **Parish Maps** pamphlets each 50p + sae.

An Introduction to the Deeds and Thoughts of Common Ground: an illustrated review of seven years work, 1990 £3.00.

Exhibitions illustrating some of Common Ground's projects including Parish Maps, New Milestones and Orchards, are available for hire. Please send sae for further details. Cheques to Common Ground. Prices include p&p.

Common Ground, 41 Shelton Street, London WC2H 9HJ
Charity registration no. 326335